MW01599312

The Spirit Of One

Kamalesh Dwivedi

कः अद्धावेद कः इह प्रवोचत् कुतः,
		आजाता कुतः इयम् विसृष्टिः
अर्वाक् देवाः अस्य विसर्जनेन,
		अथ कः वेद यतः आ बभूवः
इयम् विसृष्टि यतः आबभूव,
		यदि वा दधे यदि वा न
यः अस्य अध्यक्षः परमे व्योमन्,
		सः अंग वेद यदि वा न वेद

				-ऋग्वेद १०:१२९:६-७

Who knows the facts about creation? Who can describe it? What materials were used to create this world? Who created this? All the gods were imagined after this creation. Whence was this created, who knows? Whence did these various created beings appear, who created them or who did not create them- all this is known to only That. Or, maybe, even That does not know. सः अंग वेद यदि वा न वेद ।

				- Rigved 10:129:6-7

तस्य वाचकः प्रणवः

The Spirit of One

❖ **Published by** ❖

Atmasutra Publications
www.atmasutra.com

❖ **Printed in China** ❖

❖ **Layout, Illustratration and Cover** ❖

Mamta Dalal
www.MadARTworks.com

ISBN (10 Digit) : 0-9800029-1-5
ISBN (13 Digit) : 978-0-9800029-1-1

meditating on
Indian Saraswati, Persian Asa & Greek Athena

for

my three daughters

Swastika, Kritika, Anamika
स्वस्तिका, कृत्तिका, अनामिका

CONTENTS
सूची

Deepest Gratitude

to rishis
Vyas, Valmiki, Yagyavalkya, Patanjali

to mai
Late Shreemati Brij Kumari Dwivedi

The Spirit Of One

Epilogue
उपसंहार

One wonders whether anything has been left out from the ten spiritual dialogues presented and commented upon in previous chapters. Whether it was the dialogue between two peers, Krishna and Arjun, or the one between a husband and his wife, Yagyavalkya and Maitreyi, or the one between two rishis, Shakalya and Yagyavalkya, or the one between a man of humble beginnings and some animals, Satyakam and Rishabh, the swan and the diver-bird, or a dialogue between a son and his father, Bhrigu and Varun, it is hard to think that something has been left out. They all said, in their own ways, and they all heard, in their own ways, that there is something, inside each of us, which is indestructible, imperishable, unchanging, beyond birth, beyond death, beyond hearing, beyond sight, beyond touch, beyond taste and beyond comprehension. They called That something *Atman*, which is an emanation of something larger of the same type and which is called *Brahman*. That Brahman is everywhere. That Brahman is in everything. One who understands this will not talk about 'us versus them', will see God and Allah in everyone and in everything. Each one of us is God, who is not somewhere 'up there'. That is right here inside each of us, somewhere close to the pericardium.

However, it would be only proper to end this book with a spiritual dialogue of my own. This dialogue took place between me and one of my daughters, Kritika, in the city of Eden Prairie. While the father and the daughter were walking from the backyard of their house to the Purgatory Creek, which ran through a natural preserve, off their property,

Kritika started the conversation thus:

"Bapu, do you think whether there is a God or not?"

I responded, "I am not sure, Kriti. Christians feel, strongly, that there is a God somewhere 'up there'. The Muslims also feel there is an Allah who is also somewhere 'up there'. And…."

Kritika asked impatiently, "…and, what do the God and the Allah do?"

I responded, "I do not know. The Bible and the Koran ascribe various characteristics to their respective Beings up there. The Christians believe that everyone needs to go through Christ, their prophet from the Arabian peninsula."

"Yea, I heard, the other day, our nine year old neighbour say, 'those who do not go through Christ, they will go to hell'. I was pretty much shocked to hear that from a smart, nine year old boy, and that, too, in America, circa 2002! All of us laughed it away, even though he was serious. He also told us that that is what he has been taught in the Church."

I said, "Yeah, such talk bothers me, too. Such exclusivist viewpoints have a capacity to cause conflict and chaos……."

Kritika, then, interrupted me and turned to Koran, "I read some of the pages from the Koran on the book-shelf in the family room. They are talking about destroying idols and idol-worshippers have been called *Kafers*. Thay have also talked bad things about Jews in some *Suras*. Can all this be not edited out from the Bible and the Koran?"

I replied, "Both, the Christians and the Muslims, believe that these were 'revealed' to their respective prophets. These are, sort of, the 'word of God or Allah. It cannot be changed. Both come from the Abrahamic root and they are, both, prescriptive, exclusivist and singularist."

Kritika, then turned to Hinduism, "What do the Hindu books say? Do they have 'revealed' words, too?"

I answered, "No, there are no Hindu prophets, there are no revealed words. What we have got is a lot of books talking about thoughts of *rishis* and *munis* . Every Hindu has to seek his or her own reality. This is the 'Spirit of One'. There is no organized institution behind this 'Spirit of One'. Everyone is a seeker."

"What do they seek?"

"They try to seek whether there is something which is Time-Transcendent or not. They start with the physical realities in this world with which our sense organs interact and they progressively contemplate inwards. The goal, here, is to see whether, by pulling one's senses inwards, through the process of *Yoga*, one can realize the ultimate bliss or not. Some find it, some do not."

"What happens to those who do not find? Do they go to hell?"

We were, at this point, very close to the Purgatory Creek.

"No, they do not go to hell. They can, if they want to, start all over again in the next manifestation of the gross body form", I responded, "Seeking continues. The process, sometimes, is more pleasuresome than the end."

We stood still at the bank of the Purgatory Creek. We looked at the herd of the deer around five hundred feet away from us. We also saw some empty bird nests from the previous years and a lot of fallen geese feathers. After a while, we turned homewards.

"If someone asks you, Bapu, what comes, conceptually, closest to an idea of That, the *Brahman*, the *Atman*, the *Roh* what would you say?", asked Kritika.

"Well, this is a hard question. However, of all the physical concepts discovered so far, the idea of the Black Hole comes closest, in my view, to an idea of That, the *Brahman*."

"How do you relate a Black Hole with That?"

"As discussed in several of the dialogues, in this book, there is a thread of thought which talks about 'something' from where everything came from and 'something' by which all of the universe is sustained and then everything gets dissolved into that 'something'- that *Ishnu, Vishnu and Grasishnu* idea, Brahma, Vishnu and Mahesh, respectively. Black Hole, the mother or the father, of all gravity fits this description the closest. All matter is born of the Black Hole, through a sort of a gravitational escape, all matter is sustained through gravity and all matter goes into the Black Hole, through a gravitational collapse."

"Then, why did the scientist call it a Black Hole, implying something sinister?"

"Yea, they focused on the dissolution aspect of all matter into the Black Hole. They felt that it is something sinister, hence, the name Black Hole. However, in Veda, this has been called *Hiranya Garbha*, the Golden Womb, which is focused more on the creative aspect of the Black Hole".

"Can gravity, then, be called, That Time-Transcendent reality?", asked Kritika.

"Well, gravity comes very close to what the Indian rishis have described. They have said, *"Guru Brahma, Guru Vishnu, Guru dev Maheshwar….. gravity is Brahma, the creative force; gravity is Vishnu, the sustaining force and gravity is Mahesh(Shiva), the dissolutionary force. Guru,* in Sanskrit, means that which has the 'qualities of gravity', *gurutva.* It also means a teacher and many people translate the above quoted verse as 'the teacher is Brahma, the teacher is Vishnu' etc. I suspect the verse implies gravity and not a teacher.

"Gravity appears to have all the characteristics of the ultimate reality which has been spoken of by the rishis. Gravity is immortal, it is indestructible, it has no beginning and no end, although, it is the beginning, the middle and the end of it all. Gravity cannot be touched, smelled, seen or heard. It is everywhere, inside everything. Gravity is born of itself, it has no progenitors.

"Gravity is an irreducible reality. Time, space, heat, light, electricity and magnetism- they are all born of gravity. If there were no gravity, there will be no space, there will be no motion and there will be no time. Garvity is the Father and Mother of all. Gravity is, verily, That".

"So, how many black holes are there", asked Kritika.

As Yagyavalkya had said to Shakalya, I will say that there are three thousand three and three hundred three……. then, six, then, three and , then, one. Yeah, then, one. Because, all the black holes are connected together. One huge *Hiranya Garbha,* indeed, the great Golden Womb", I replied.

"Bapu, how does one become immortal?"

"By having children of your own and they having their own children and their children having children and thus it goes on and on……..genes never die, if this happens".

The discussion had, indeed, become *guru*, heavy. We had almost reached our backyard.

It was my turn now, I asked her a question, "So, do you understand what is That?"

"Yeah, sort of", replied Kritika, "but I will continue my own seeking when I grow older".

"That is The Spirit of One! There are no final words in spiritual seeking. Ignorance and dishonesty can persuade some to claim that their view is the only view and, also, the final view. Only fools and fanatics have final words".

"Let's go in and make a *chai* for Bapu as a *guru-dakshina*, a teacher's fee", I said, teasingly. We, both, had tea in the family room.

Thus came to an end a spiritual dialogue between a father and his daughter as they walked from their backyard to the Purgatory Creek and back home.

Arjun-Krishna Dialogue
Preface (भूमिका)

The dialogue between Arjun and Krishna took place in 1478 BC, with a margin of error of one year, as discovered by Professor R. N. Iyengar of the Indian Institute of Science, Bangalore. This date, however, is disputed by other researchers who say that the current age, Kali Yuga, started in 3102 BC and the Mahabharat war took place in the age before the Kali Yuga, the Dwapar Yuga. Therefore, they claim, the Mahabharat war happened some time before 3102 BC. It is obvious that more research is required. Whatever the historicity of this dialogue, it best illustrates the premise behind and the promise of 'The Spirit of One'. As one goes through this dialogue, one discovers that a process, which is repeatable in nature, has been laid out by Krishna. Using this process of Nishkam Karma Yoga, a person can realize the highest point of the spiritual quest. No blind faith is either demanded or commanded by Krishna as he leads Arjun on his spiritual journey. Arjun-Krishna dialogue is also important because it has been presented in the Bhagavad Gita, simply known as the Gita, which has come to be regarded as the quintessential summary of the upanishadic thought.

The context for this dialogue is the beginning of the Mahabharat war when the armies of Pandavas and Kauravas were facing each other in the battlefield of Kurukshetra, which is located northwest of modern day New Delhi in India. The war was about to start. A roll call had been just completed and every known commander and warrior of the time was present in battle fatigue and was aligned either on the Pandavas' side or on the Kauravas'. Before the battle began, Arjun got besieged with a reluctance to fight in the war. After seeing his cousins and teachers facing him on the opposite side of the battlefield, Arjun says:

दृष्ट्वा इमान् स्वजनान् कृष्ण युयुत्सून् समवस्थितान्
सीदन्ति मम गात्राणि मुखम् च परिशुष्यति (१:२८)

"Krishna, the sight of my own people, who are assembled here to fight, is making my limbs give up and making my mouth dry up." Arjun is trembling and is feeling dehydrated. He further goes on making statements like these:

निमित्तानि च पश्यामि विपरीतानि केशवः (१:३०)

न च श्रेयः अनुपश्यामि हत्वा स्वजनं आहवे
न कांक्षे विजयं कृष्ण न च राज्यं सुखानि च (१:३१)

किं नो राज्येन गोविन्द किं भोगैः जीवितेन वा
येषां अर्थे कांक्षितं नो राज्यं भोगाः सुखानि च (१:३२)

ते इमे अवस्थिता युद्धे प्राणान् त्यक्त्वा धनानि च
आचार्याः पितरः पुत्राः तथा एव च पितामहाः (१:३३)

मातुलाः श्वशुराः पौत्राः श्यालाः सम्बन्धिनः तथा
एतान् न हन्तुं इच्छामि घ्नतः अपि मधुसूदनः (१:३४)

"Krishna, not only that, I am having all the bad omens. After the war is over and is won by us, what will I do with a kingdom, what will I do with my life, and what will I do with all the enjoyments of life? Those for whom I wish the enjoyment of life and those for whom I wish the pleasures of life, all of them- my teachers, uncles, nephews, grandparents, mother's brothers, father-in-laws, brother-in-laws, the grand nephews and other relatives- are lined up for a war and are ready to sacrifice their lives and their wealth. Krishna, even if they hurt me, I am not going to fight, hurt and kill them!" As one can see, Arjun has resolved not to fight. He seems to have concluded that 'even though my opponents are ready to hurt and, possibly, kill me, I am not going to kill them'. एतान् न हन्तुं इच्छामि घ्नतः अपि मधुसूदनः (१:३८)।

He appears to be so resolved as not to fight in the war that he further strengthens his position by saying:

अपि त्रैलोक्य राज्यस्य हेतोः किं न महीकृते
निहत्य धार्तराष्ट्रान् नः का प्रीतिः स्यात् जनार्दनः (१:३५)

"Krishna, even if we gain, as a result of our victory, not only the earth but also the three worlds- the temporal world, the time transcendent world and the world in btween (मनुष्यलोक, देवलोक, पितृलोक) - what kind of gain that would be after killing the children of my own uncle, Dhritarashtra?" स्वजनं हि कथं हत्वा सुखिनः स्याम् माधव (१:३६) 'How shall we be happy by killing our own people' seems to be bothering Arjun. He, then, goes on explaining his position to Krishna who had been quietly and patiently listening to the process of rationalization Arjun was going through for his reluctance to go to war. Arjun finally puts down his bow and arrows and sits down on the chariot, which was being commanded by Krishna.

Krishna feels that there is some room for maneuver for his peer-leadership skills. He noticed that Arjun had moved away from a rigid position like – 'even though they are ready to hurt me I am not going to kill them' एतान् न हन्तुं इच्छामि

ध्वनतः अपि मधुसूदनः (१:३७)- to a question when he put down his bow and arrows- 'How shall we be happy by killing our own people (१:३६) ?' Arjun seems to have given some room, indeed, by moving away from a somewhat harder resolve to a question, although a difficult one.

Krishna has a tough job at hand. He has to quickly design a strategy to bring Arjun out of his predicament and to convince him to go to war. Krishna has to shake away the soft sentimentality which has overtaken Arjun. The question is: how does Krishna go about achieving this objective? He could have said, "Believe me, I am your great friend, trust me, let's go to war". A swearing by the greatness of their mutual friendship would have proven to be an inadequate reason for a man who had, among other things, earlier said, 'even in exchange for the three worlds (मनुष्यलोक,पितृलोक,देवलोक), I would not fight "अपि त्रैलोक्य राज्यस्य हेतोः किं न महीकृते । To respond to a tough situation at hand, Krishna's leadership skills, as we will see later, will be deployed to the fullest extent.

Krishna starts with laying out a vision for life, a vision for life before life and and a vision for life after life. All these three visions seem different, but they are connected with one vision of temporal transcendence. His strategy is based upon three key elements- (1) A vision of *Atman*, the time transcendent self, (2) An approach of *Nishkam Karma,* utmost professionalism, and (3) A follow-up through *Bhakti*, a complete trust in the leader. These three elements can be compared with elements of modern day concepts about leadership, which is based upon: (1) A vision for the future, (2) A professional execution and (3) A reposition of trust in the leadership. A vision clearly states that which is beyond the immediate, beyond the comfort zone and conjures up and communicates images of what the future would look like. Then, a call to professionalism- detached execution, a sense of duty detached from the outcome of a series of steps to be taken to accomplish the goals- is issued to achieve the vision. Trust and confidence in the leadership is a necessary ingredient along the way.

Atman, Nishkam Karma and *Bhakti*- these are the three key concepts Krishna lays out in front of Arjun in the Gita. He also deploys Yoga as an aid to execute Nishkam Karma, professionalism unattached to the outcome of one's actions. While Krishna is engaged in a serious dialogue with Arjun, Arjun asks/raises sixteen questions/issues as presented in the Gita. These sixteen questions/issues and Krishna's response to them form a foundation for Arjun's spiritual quest and progression from a temporal world to a time transcendent world. Arjun's spiritual journey takes him through an understanding of the nature of self and, also, the nature of nature itself. These three core concepts of Atman, Nishkam Karma and Bhakti have been briefly introduced below.

Atman (आत्मन):

Krishna, in a very clever way, built a vision for Arjun based upon one of the core concepts of Indian spirituality- Atman. This concept had already been alluded to and expounded upon, in great depth, before the Mahabharat war, in texts like Vedas, Upanishads and Smritis. Atman is a seminal spiritual concept buried very deep in an Indian psyche for more than ten thousand years of continuous civilization. Atman is, sometimes, translated as 'soul' in English. This translation must be viewed with great caution as the word, soul, has a very specific and different import in some religions. A word which is much more closer to the concept of Atman is the Persian word- Roh (रोह), which is derived from the Sanskrit root Ruh (रुह्), meaning that which ascends (आरोहति).

As mentioned earlier, Arjun's desire for not fighting his own kith and kin in the impending war is based upon his concern for destruction and killing of his relatives. His idea of life seems to be a life which begins at the moment of conception, subsequent birth and which ends with death. This concept of life has an inherent assumption, which is built around a view which has a past, a present and a future. Whatever is present, now, in its current form was not like it in the past. Whatever is present, now, in its current form will cease to be in the future if the current form is destroyed. In this model of life, there is nothing which is always present, which is always in its present state- in the past as well as in the future. There is nothing which can transcend destruction of its form. There is nothing which always lives in the present, because the present is too short-very similar to a mathematical singularity, a sort of temporal discontinuity. What was there in the past and what will be there in the future and what is at time 't=0' does not exist. The present, time 't=0', extended in both temporal directions, does not exist in Arjun's model of life.

Through the concept of Atman, Krishna introduces the concept of 'ever present-ness', something which has no past and something which will have no future and something which lives in the present forever. *This, which lives at time 't=0', forever, is Atman.* Atman extends and transforms the temporal discontinuity at time 't=0' to a state of timelessness where there is no past and there is no future. Only thing which is there is the Time itself and not its measure. When the measure of time is removed from the model of life, when the past and the future are discarded, then, the only thing, which remains, is the present, the ever-present, the Atman. This concept resembles what is called the scientific black hole, which does no get born, which does not grow older and which does not die. It is just there. It always lives on.

Krishna lays out this vision of an ever-present Atman in a very confident and, also, in a very clever way through metaphors and examples. Let's see how he puts it, in his own words:

अशोच्यान् अनुअशोच: त्वं प्रज्ञावादान् च भाषसे
गतासून् अगतासून् च न अनुशोचन्ति पण्डिताः (२:११)

"Arjun, you are worried about things not worth worrying about. And you are, at the same time, sounding like a wise man! To the contrary, wise people do not worry for those who are living and, also, for those who are dead." Krishna is implying that getting attached to something which is, by its very nature, prone to destruction and change is not worth worrying about. He further adds:

न तु एव अहं जातु न आसं न त्वं न इमे जनाधिपाः
न च एव न भविष्यामः सर्वे वयम् अतः परम् (२:१२)

"There was not a time when I was not present and you were not present and these kings were not present. There will never be a time, in the future, when all of us will not be!" Through this statement Krishna begins to point towards something which, he believes, is ever-present; which lives at time 't=0' extended in both temporal directions and which transcends measurement of time. Let's look at some more elaboration from Krishna:

मात्रास्पर्शाः तु कौन्तेय शीतोष्ण सुखदुःखदाः
आगमापायिनः अनित्याः तान् तितिक्षस्व भारतः (२:१४)

ना असतो विद्यते भावो न अभावो विद्यते सतः
उभयोः अपि दृष्टः अन्तः तु अनयोः तत्त्वं दर्शिभिः (२:१६)

अविनाशि तु तत् विद्धि येन सर्वम् इदं ततम्
विनाशम् अव्ययस्य अस्य न कश्चित् कर्तुं अर्हति (२:१७)

"Arjun, because of the sense organs and the objects of these sense organs, people feel pain and pleasure. The pain and the pleasure, by themselves, are short-lived and they last as long as the sense organs are in a temporal or spatial proximity with their sense-objects. Deal with them, Arjun. If the existence of something, for example, pain and pleasure, depends upon the sense organs coming into close temporal or spatial proximity with their sense-objects, then, that thing does not have an independent existence and, therefore, does not exist (असत् है). That whose existence does not depend upon a temporal or spatial proximity between the sense organs and their objects is the one which always exists (सत् है). That which is everywhere in this body is the one which is beyond death and destruction. No one can destroy that which is indestructible: विनाशम् अव्ययस्य अस्य न कश्चित् कर्तुं अर्हति (२:१७)!"

As one can see, Krishna is becoming more and more assertive in his formulation for something which is indestructible and which is ever-present; which has no past and no future in terms of temporal measurement but that is there in the past as well as in the future. *This is the concept of ever-present Atman, extension of the temporal discontinuity at time 't=0' in both directions.* Krishna does not stop here:

य एनं वेत्ति हन्तारं यः च एनं मन्यते हतम्
उभौ तौ न विजानितो न अयं हन्ति न हन्यते (२:१९)

"Those who mistake this Atman for that which destroys or for that which gets destroyed, they, both, do not know. This Atman neither kills someone nor gets killed by anyone." Furthermore, Krishna goes on characterizing Atman as that which is beyond birth, beyond death, beyond destruction and which is 'just simply always there'. That is present everywhere; that is beyond change and that is beyond measure of change. Despite laying down this vision of Atman for Arjun, Krishna argues that "even if you consider this Atman getting born and subsequently dying, then, why do you worry about killing others? They will be re-born again, anyway (२:२६,२:२७)! All life forms are unexpressed (अव्यक्त) and unmanifest before birth and they become unexpressed, again, after death. They are in an 'expressed' (व्यक्त), manifest state, between birth and death. Therefore, O Arjun, there should be no reason for your predicament (२:२८)."

What a masterful vision Krishna laid out for a person who is hesitant to go to a lawful and just war due to his concern for killing his own kith and kin? The construction of the concept of Atman has paved the way for Krishna to lead Arjun to the next stage, which is the stage of *Nishkam Karma* (निष्काम कर्म).

Nishkam Karma (निष्काम कर्म):

After giving a strong indication that there is something which is beyond destruction and which is beyond birth and death, Krishna encourages Arjun, for the war, thus:

हतो वा प्राप्स्यसि स्वर्गं जित्वा वा भोक्ष्यसे महीम्
तस्माद् उतिष्ठ कौन्तेय युद्धाय कृत निश्चयः (२:३७)

"Arjun, suppose, for a moment, that you die in the battlefield. If that happens, you will go to swarg. And, suppose, that you win in the battlefield. If that happens, you will rule the world. Therefore, stand up and fight with an unwavering determination." This is Krishna's clarion call to Arjun to come out of his predicament; this is Krishna's call to Arjun for action. It is a win-win situation, either way, whether Arjun wins in the war or he dies in the war. If he gets killed in the war, he will go to Swarg, a place where 'there is no fear, there is no old age, there is neither hunger nor thirst and where there are no worries and where there is all bliss' (स्वर्गलोके न भयम् किम् च नास्ति, न तत्र त्वम् न जरया बिभेति, उभे तीत्वा अशनाया पिपासे, शोकातिगो मोदते स्वर्गलोके (१:१:१२, कठोपनिषद). If he wins, he will enjoy the pleasures of this very world. He further lays out the key points of the second leg of his strategy, just in case if Arjun missed the whole point about Atman.

सुखदुःखे समे कृत्वा लाभ अलाभौ जय अजयौ
ततो युद्धाय युज्यस्व न एवं पापं अवाप्स्यसि (२:३८)

"In happiness and sadness, in victory and defeat and in gain and loss- under all these circumstances- keep a steady mind. Therefore, get engaged in the act of a lawful and just war,

Arjun. And you will not be accused of 'not performing your professional duties' (पापम्). This is the foundational statement for the second leg of Krishna's strategy. This statement sows the seeds of the concept of *Nishkam Karma*. Krishna was concerned that Arjun might not have grasped the full import of the concept of Atman, the concept of freezing and extension of time 't=0' in both temporal directions. In the second part of his strategy, he is trying to detach Arjun's mind from the outcome of his actions and, also, from the process of executing his actions, a core basis of modern day professionalism. One of the most often quoted statements of Krishna goes like this:

कर्मणि एव अधिकार: ते मा फलेषु कदाचन
मा कर्मफलं हेतु: भू: मा ते सङ्ग: अस्तु अकर्मणि (२:४७)

"Arjun, do your professional duties (कर्म as contrasted with अकर्म and विकर्म). Do not get attached to the outcome of your professional duties. You must not ascribe the cause of your duties to yourself, nor should you allow yourself to be beset with 'not doing the professional duties' (अकर्म)". This statement is a good example of what is now known as a professional approach in one's work in modern day management practices. Nishkam Karma demands highest order of professionalism, where there is no room for not performing one's duties according to one's profession; where there is no room for attachment to the process of execution of one's duties. Those who get attached to the outcome of their duties have been called *Kripana* (कृपण), an object of utter sympathy. "कृपणा: फलहेतव:", that is the way Krishna calls people who get attached to the outcome of their duties (२:४९). Krishna wants Arjun to perform his *Kshatra Dharma*

(क्षात्र धर्म), which has been cross-generationally handed down to him, in a professional manner. He is a warrior, his father was a warrior, his grandfather was a warrior and so on. There must not be any room for vacillation while conducting a warrior's duties (क्षात्र धर्म). He says thus:

स्वधर्ममम् अपि च अवेक्ष्य न विकम्पितुम् अर्हसि
धर्मात् हि युद्धात् श्रेयः अन्यत् क्षत्रियस्य न विद्यते (२:३१)

"If you look at your cross-generational duties of a warrior, it is not appropriate to vacillate in the battlefield. Because, for a Kshatriya, there is nothing superior to going to a lawful and just war." He adds, furthermore, to emphasize his point:

सुखिनः क्षत्रियाः पार्थ लभन्ते युद्धम् इदृशम् (२:३२)

"Only fortunate *Kshatriyas* get an opportunity, like this one, to fight in a just and a lawful war." Krishna implies that an opportunity of a lifetime is knocking at Arjun's doors and he must not let it go by without exploiting it. This sounds like an exhortation from a leader to his troops in the battlefield.

A question arises as to what are the ways and the means by which a state of Nishkam Karma can be achieved? How can one carry out one's duties without getting attached to the outcome? How is that possible? How is that attainable? Let's see what advice the leader has:

मात्रास्पर्शाः तु कौन्तेय शीतोष्ण सुखदुःखदाः
आगमापायिनः अनित्याः तान् तितिक्षस्व भारत: (२:१४)

"Arjun, because of the contact of sense organs with their objects, people feel pain and pleasure. The pain or the pleasure, by itself, is short-lived. They, both, last as long as the sense organs are in temporal or spatial contact with their objects. Deal with them, Arjun." On how to attain a state of Nishkam Karma, Krishna advises thus:

यदा संहरते च अयम् कर्मोऽङ्गान् इव सर्वशः
इन्द्रियाणि इन्द्रियार्थेभ्यः तस्य प्रज्ञा प्रतिष्ठिता (२:५८)

"A turtle, by its own reflexes, retracts its limbs away from the sense objects. Likewise, if a person can do the same, then, that person's mind is said to have transitioned to a state of *Pragya Pratistha* (प्रज्ञा प्रतिष्ठा)", which is a necessary and an intermediate step towards attaining a state of Nishkam Karma. Incidentally, this is also one of the statements Krishna has made in response to the first question of Arjun, which will be covered in detail in Chapter-I. It will, however, be sufficient to note here that *Pragya Pratistha* is a characteristic of a Yogic meditative state and Yoga is a major tool to attain the state of *Nishkam Karma*.

Bhakti (भक्ति):

Let's suppose, for a moment, that Arjun is unable to grasp the subtleness of the concept of Atman and its nature of indestructibility and unchangeability and its quality of being beyond birth and death. Let's, again, suppose that Arjun is unable to execute his cross-generational duties in a way that is detached from its outcome and, also, detached from the process to reach the outcome in a professional manner. Let's say, he cannot attain a state of Nishkam Karma. What happens, then? Well, he will be, in the worst case, where he was, at the very start, even after a considerable effort made by Krishna in laying down the two legs of his three pronged strategy. Krishna is aware of this and, therefore, he proceeds to the third element of his strategy, which is the concept of *Bhakti* (भक्ति). Bhakti is, simply stated in modern terms, a complete reposition of trust in one's leader and the leadership skills. If everything else fails- if the concept of Atman is too complex and too subtle to grasp and the concept of Nishkam Karma is too demanding for an ordinary mortal like Arjun to practise, then, the leader must have a great resume so as to be able to command a complete reposition of trust in his abilities to lead. Let's look at some of the items in Krishna's resume as he has stated:

अहम्   आत्मा   गुडाकेश   सर्वभूताशयस्थितः
अहम् आदिः च मध्यम् च भूतानाम् अन्त एव च (१०:२०)

"Arjun, I am the Atman in every living being. I am the cause of birth, existence and death of all beings". Furthermore, the resume reads:

वेदानाम् सामवेदः अस्मि देवानाम्   अस्मि वासवः
इन्द्रियाणाम् मनः च अस्मि भूतानाम् अस्मि चेतना (१०:२२)

अश्वत्थः सर्ववृक्षाणाम्   देवर्षीणाम्   च   नारदः
गन्धर्वाणाम् चित्ररथः सिद्धानाम् कपिलः मुनिः (१०:२६)

"Among the Vedas, I am the Sam Ved (सामवेद), I am Indra among the Sur, I am the very consciousness in the body. Furthermore, I am the Pipal tree among the trees and Narad (नारद) among the rishis, among the Gandharvas I am Chitrarath and I am Kapil muni among those who have attained Pragya Pratistha (प्रज्ञा प्रतिष्ठा)." After giving a great detail about his abilities by identifying himself with the very best there is, he finally says:

सर्गाणाम् आदिः अन्तः च मध्यम् च एव अहम् अर्जुन (१०:३२)

"Arjun, I am the beginning, the middle and the end of it all which exists", thus declares Krishna. 'सृज्यन्त इति सर्गा', all that which exists is called *sarga* (सर्ग). Krishna seems to have taken a long leap from affirming 'I am the cause of the beginning, the end and everything in between for every living being to 'I am the beginning, the middle and the end of it all which exists'. Who would not like to have a leader like Krishna, then? His great resume will certainly command Arjun's trust and respect. Indeed, Krishna is no ordinary charioteer in the battlefield.

These three concepts of *Atman, Nishkam Karma* and *Bhakti* are key concepts in the process of unique spiritual experience for each person. The challenge is how to reach a state when the indestructibility of Atman can be realized. Once this realization occurs, then, the universality of Atman can also be experienced. When that happens, then, each seeker can rightfully claim, 'I am That, I am That'. And, that is the experience and the promise of 'The Spirit of One', which will be expanded upon in succeeding chapters.

Chapter I
The First Question of Arjun

अर्जुनस्य प्रथमः प्रश्नः

It has been mentioned earlier that *Pragya Pratistha* (प्रज्ञा प्रतिष्ठा) is a necessary and a first step towards attaining a state of *Nishkam Karma*. *Pragya Pratistha* is also a characteristic of a *Yogic* meditative state and *Yoga* is a major tool to attain the state of *Nishkam Karma*, which, in turn, is a necessary step to be taken on the path of spiritual awakening. A person who has reached this state is called a *Sthit-Pragya*(स्थितप्रज्ञ) person. Arjun's first question to Krishna is to know, in detail, what is *Pragya Pratistha* and how to attain this state. He asks,

स्थितप्रज्ञस्य का भाषा समाधिस्थस्य केशव
स्थितधीः किं प्रभाषेत किम् आसीत व्रजेत किम् (२:५४)

"Krishna, what are the characteristics of a *Sthit-Pragya* (स्थितप्रज्ञ) person? What does a Sthit-Pragya person talk about ? How does that person sit and walk ?" In simple words, Arjun's first question to Krishna is, 'How does one characterize a *Sthit-Pragya* (स्थितप्रज्ञ) person?' This is an important question whose answer will take a person towards Nishkam Karma and, ultimately, towards realizing the true nature of Atman itself. We will consider Krishna's responses to this question and construct an understanding of what is Sthit-Pragya. Pragya Pratistha (प्रज्ञा प्रतिष्ठा) has been briefly mentioned, before, in the preface. Krishna has stated that "I am Kapil muni among those who have attained Pragya Pratistha (प्रज्ञा प्रतिष्ठा). सिद्धानाम् कपिलः मुनिः (१०:२६)." He has further said that: इन्द्रियाणि इन्द्रियार्थेभ्यः तस्य प्रज्ञा प्रतिष्ठिता (२:५८)

"A turtle, by its own its own reflexes, retracts its limbs away from the sense objects. Likewise, if a person can do the same, then, that person's mind is said to have transitioned to a state of *Pragya Pratistha* (प्रज्ञा प्रतिष्ठा)", which is a necessary step towards attainment of the state of Nishkam Karma. Let's see what Krishna says further:

प्रजहाति यदा कामान् सर्वान् पार्थ मनोगतान्
आत्मनि एव आत्मना तुष्टः स्थितप्रज्ञः तदा उच्यते (२:५५)

"Arjun, when a person relinquishes all desires (कामान् सर्वान्) and is content with one's own self, then, that person is said to have reached the stage of Sthit-Pragya (स्थितप्रज्ञ)." The implication of this response is that when the relationship between the sense organs and the sense objects is well managed and, perhaps, well controlled, then, it is possible to feel totally contented with one's own self. A person, then, is drawn towards one's own self and ultimately becomes one with one's self. Kath Upanishad (कठोपनिषद) also supports this:

यदा सर्वे प्रमुच्यन्ते कामा ये अस्य हृदि स्थिताः
अथ मर्त्यः अमृतः भवति यत्र ब्रह्म समश्नुते (२३:१८)

When all desires leave a person's heart, then, even a mortal being acquires immortality and realizes Brahman (ब्रह्मन्, ब्रह्म), the ultimate reality, the ultimate truth. By saying कामान् सर्वान् मनोगतान् (all desires have left the mind) Krishna implies, through the qualifier मनोगतान् (have left the mind), that it is possible for desires to leave the mind. Desires and a person's mind do not have the same relationship as fire has with heat or heat has with light. Therefore, it is possible for a person to relinquish desires. In other words, for a person to have desires is not as natural as for fire to have heat or for heat to have light. The relationship between a person's mind and one's desires is called un-natural, relinquishable relationship, अनात्म धर्म (*Anatma Dharma*), whereas that between fire and heat, for example, is called natural, unrelinquishable relationship आत्म धर्म (*Atma Dharma*). Due to this relationship of *anatmatva* (अनात्मत्व) between the mind and desires, it is in the realm of possibility to relinquish all desires and reach a state where a person is content with one's own self (आत्मनि एव आत्मना तुष्टः २:५५). Some of the characteristics of a person who has reached the state of Sthit-Pragya (स्थितप्रज्ञ) have also been described by Krishna thus:

दुःखेषु   अन   उद्विग्नमनाः   सुखेषु   विगतस्पृहः
वीतरागभयक्रोधः   स्थितधीः   मुनिः   उच्यते (२:५६)
अथच,
यः   सर्वत्र   अनभिस्नेहः   तत् तत् प्राप्य   शुभ   अशुभम्
न   अभिनन्दति   न   द्वेष्टि   तस्य   प्रज्ञा   प्रतिष्ठिता (२:५७)

*"Those who do not get moved even in great adversity and those who become desire less in times of great wealth and those who do not have attachment, fear and anger (*राग भय क्रोध*)- they are called Sthit-Pragya* (स्थितप्रज्ञ). And more, "Sthit-Pragya (स्थितप्रज्ञ) are those who do not get excessively attached to worldly possessions and pleasures and those who do not become excessively happy after getting desired objects; nor do they become excessively sad upon not getting desired objects". The question arises, now, how does one reach to a state of mind like this? We sort of get an idea about some of the characteristics of a Sthit-Pragya (स्थितप्रज्ञ) person, the person who can manage one's desires well, whose desires are not running amock and the desires are under the firm control of one's wisdom (बुद्धि) and that person does not get overly excited either in adversity or in happiness. The question, now, is how to get there? Krishna uses the previously stated

metaphor, at the cost of being repetitive, to drive the point home:

यदा संहरते च अयम् कूर्मोऽङ्गान इव सर्वशः
इन्द्रियाणि इन्द्रियार्थेभ्यः तस्य प्रज्ञा प्रतिष्ठिता (२:५८)

"A turtle, by its own reflexes, retracts its limbs away from the sense objects. Likewise, if a person can do the same, then, that person's mind is said to have transitioned to a state of *Pragya Pratistha* (प्रज्ञा प्रतिष्ठा)", a necessary step towards a state of Nishkam Karma. As Krishna explains further, loosening the knot which ties a person's mind to one's desires is only the first step to be taken to become a Sthit-Pragya (स्थितप्रज्ञ) person. A mere physical separation between sense organs and their sense objects is not enough. A physical separation is good and desired, however, a mental separation- a sense of detachment- is a must. Illustratively, it is not enough to keep fire away from a bundle of dry woods. Fire will reach the bundle of dry woods as long as there is a link between the two through a trail of tiny, dry grass blades. Therefore, it is essential to remove all such tiny grass blades from the trail to prevent the fire from reaching the bundle of dry woods. It is, likewise, necessary to sever the mental attachment from the sense objects, because:

यततो हि अपि कौन्तेय पुरुषस्य विपश्चितः
इन्द्रियाणि प्रमाथीनि हरन्ति प्रसभम् मनः (२:६०)

"The sense organs, if not well managed and controlled, are able to overwhelm even the most rational mind." वशे हि यस्य इन्द्रियाणि तस्य प्रज्ञा प्रतिष्ठिता (२:६१), this is the way Krishna concludes, 'one whose sense organs are firmly under one's control is the person who can be called a Sthit-Pragya (स्थितप्रज्ञ) person'.

Mind is a good starting place, as Krishna has alluded to, in controlling one's sense organs. If a person's mind keeps constantly thinking of objects of senses, then, this very thinking, which is a mental process, becomes the cause of attachment (आसक्ति) to the sense objects. Mental attachment to a sense object gives rise to a desire (काम) to acquire that sense object. If that desire is not fulfilled, then, that results in

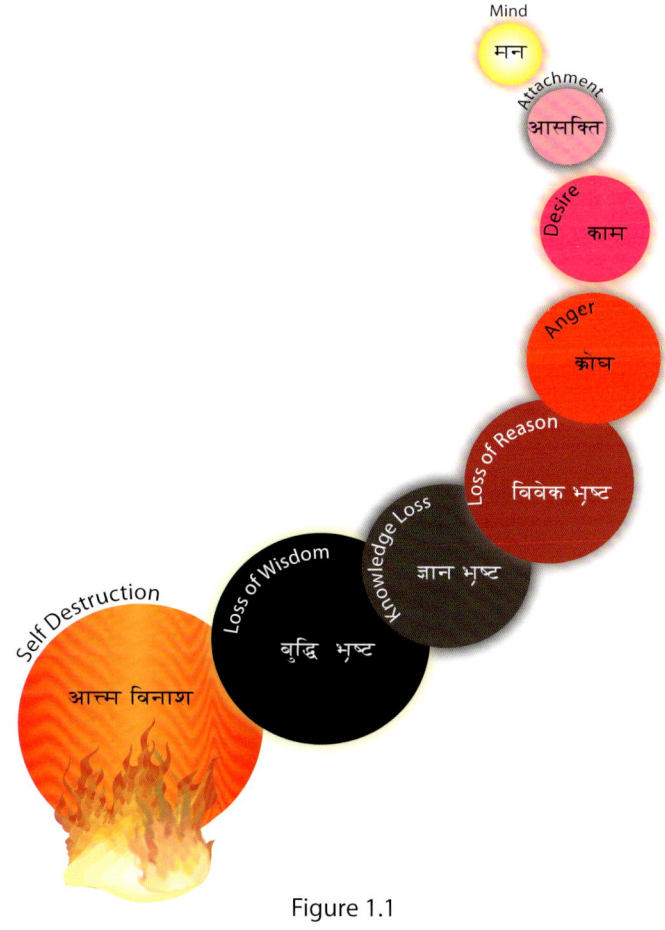

Figure 1.1

anger (क्रोध). Anger, in turn, weakens and, subsequently, takes away one's reasoning power (विवेक). After reasoning power goes away, then, a state of what to do and what not do sets in which results in a loss of memory for great teachings of past seers. Following this, wisdom gets destroyed and, then, a person becomes as good as a dead person even though one may be physically alive. This step-by-step reasoning, by Krishna, has been presented in Figure: 1-1.

Mind, when it gets excessively attached to sense objects, ultimately leads to a person's self-destruction through the intermediate steps of desire, anger, loss of reason, loss of knowledge and loss of wisdom. This escalatory process is akin to a chemical chain reaction. Therefore, one way to control sense organs and to maintain a healthy relationship between sense organs and sense objects is to redirect the mind away from, almost always, 'voting' for the sense-organs and towards 'listening' more to the intellect and one's wisdom. When the mind gets redirected in this way, then, the steps, which lead to self-destruction, do not set in. Krishna says:

विहाय कामान् यः सर्वान् पुमान् चरति निःस्पृहः
निर्ममो निरहङ्कारः सः शान्तिम् अधिगच्छति (२:७१)

"Those who lead a life which is free of desires, destructive ego and attachment to sense objects, they, truly, attain peace of mind". *This end-state of a Sthit-Pragya* (स्थितप्रज्ञ) *person's mind is also called Brahmi-Sthiti* (ब्राह्मी स्थिति). Krishna further extols the virtue of a Sthit-Pragya (स्थितप्रज्ञ) mind :

स्थित्वा अस्यां अन्तकाले अपि ब्रह्म निर्वाणम् ऋच्छति (२:७२)

A person who, even for a moment, attains this state of *Brahmi-Sthiti* (ब्राह्मी स्थिति), even while in one's death bed, that person attains the state of complete *Brahm-Nirvana* (ब्रह्म निर्वाण॔. In Maitrayani Upanishad (मैत्रायणि उपनिषद), a rishi says,

मन एव मनुष्याणाम् कारणम् बन्ध मोक्षयो:
बन्धाय विषयासक्तम् मुक्त्यै निर्विषयम् स्मृतिम् इति (८:११)

Verily, it is the mind (मन) which is the cause for a person's attachment (बन्धन) and unattachment (मोक्ष) to this world. Attachment brings excessive interest in the objects of sense organs, whereas 'unattachment to the objects of sense organs' (निर्विषयम्) brings true freedom (मुक्ति). It is a very important step in the process of spiritual realization to understand the relative importance of mind and how it works. Once it is understood that it is the mind which keeps us embroiled in worldly pursuits beyond the fullfilment of our genuine and critical needs and keeps us away from reaching the realm of Atman and to Brahman, then, it becomes an issue of focus on the right thing. Mind needs to be turned inwards and away from an excessive attachment to the working of sense organs and their objects. Arjun is being led, progressively, from an understanding of this rudimentary but fundamental reality to higher levels of awakening, to intellect, wisdom and, ultimately, Atman, itself. On the road to experience 'The Spirit of One', understanding the mind and its relationship to the world is an important step. It is especially true in the context of the bazaar, the world, *the donya*, where there are, now, literally hundreds of thousands of sense objects vying with each other for a tiny space in a person's mind and for their subsequent attachment to the neuronal nodes.

Chapter II
The Second Question of Arjun

अर्जुनस्य द्वितीयः प्रश्नः

While Krishna was explaining to Arjun the relationship of the mind to sense organs and the relationship of sense organs to sense objects, he may not have realized that Arjun's mind was also at work. Arjun had been thinking that the verb between the sense organs and the sense objects is the one whch needs to be severed. In his mind, if no one does any work, then there will be little room for sense organs to satiate themselves with sense objects, because some work is required to bring them in close temporal and spatial proximity to each other. Therefore, he concludes that '*no karma, no attachment*'! However, before he firms it up in his mind, he asks his spiritual peer and guide the second question:

ज्यायसी चेत कर्मणः ते मता बुद्धिः जनार्दन
तत् किं कर्मणि घोरे मां नियोजयसि केशव (३:१)

"Krishna, if wisdom is more desirable than Karma (कर्म), then, why are you asking me to engage in this awful act of war ?", questions Arjun. This is a great question from a warrior, clad in a battle fatigue, who sees his kith and kin, lined up against him, for a destructive war and as he is beset with a predicament whether he should really go to war or not. Why should he not detach himself from all this cataclysmic 'nonsense' and from the potential gains from the war whether he gets killed in the war or wins the war? As Krishna had earlier said, हतो वा प्राप्यसि स्वर्गं जित्वा वा भोक्ष्यसे महीम्(२:३७) 'if you get killed in the war you will go to *swarg,* on the other hand, if you win the war you will rule the earth!' Why should Arjun not get mentally detached from all this victory and defeat? Why should he engage in the bloodshed and that, too, of his own kith and kin? Why should he not try to attain *Brahmi-Sthiti*(ब्राह्मी स्थिति) and a complete Brahm-Nirvana(ब्रह्म निर्वाण)? In his response to the first question, Krishna had emphasized that the relationship between the sense organs and sense objects must be managed carefully and that mind must not be allowed to fall prey to sense objects. Mind must supervise sense organs and not the other way around; intellect must manage the mind and wisdom must lead the intellect as shown in Figure: 2.1.

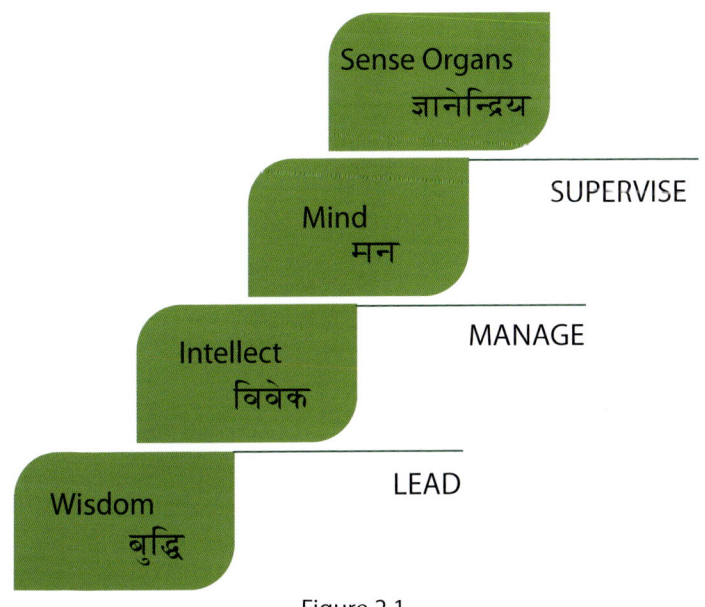

Figure 2.1

Then, why Krishna is exhorting Arjun, "Get up, with great determination, and fight the war " उतिष्ठ कौन्तेय युद्धाय कृत निश्चयः (२:३७)? In the model, as shown in Figure 2.1 which depicts the structural relationship between wisdom, intellect, mind and the sense organs, wisdom is the supreme leader. If Arjun follows up on Krishna's response to the first question and engages himself in becoming a *Sthit-Pragya* (स्थितप्रज्ञ) person and, therefore, remains unmoved by either misery or mirth, then, logically, there is no need for him to go to war. It was true that the Kauravas, his cousins, had been worse than unkind to the Pandavas. It was true that half of the kingdom of Hastinapur lawfully belonged to the Pandavas. It was also true that the Kauravas refused to part with even five villages for Pandavas. It is indeed a great adversity and suffering which has befallen the Pandavas. However, one of the things Krishna had said in his response to the first question is this: विहाय कामान् यः सर्वान् पुमान् चरति निःस्पृहः, निर्ममो निरहङ्कारः सः शान्तिम् अधिगच्छति (२:७१) "Those who lead a life which is free from desires, destructive ego and attachment to sense objects, they, truly, attain peace of mind". Then, Arjun asks, "Why do you want me to go to war?" Arjun feels utterly confused. He cannot figure out what to do when he asks Krishna,

तत् एकम् वद निश्चित्य येन श्रेयः अहम् आप्नुयाम् (३:२)

'Tell me the one, with certainty, which is really a good thing to do? Should I be unattached, unmoved, unagitated at all the injustice meted out to us by Kauravas or should I go to war to avenge all this'? Krishna finds some room for further explanation:

लोके अस्मिन् द्विविधा निष्ठा पुरा प्रोक्ता मया अनघ ज्ञानयोगेन सांख्यानाम् कर्मयोगेन योगिनाम् (३:३)

अथ च,
न कर्मणाम् अनारम्भात् नैष्कर्म्यं पुरुषः अश्नुते
न च संन्यसनात् एव सिद्धिं समधिगच्छति (३:४)

"Arjun, as I have said before, there are two major paths in this world en route to become *Sthit-Pragya*(स्थितप्रज्ञ) and to attain *Brahmi-Sthiti* (ब्राह्मी स्थिति) and, subsequently, a complete *Brahm-Nirvana* (ब्रह्म निर्वाण). One path is for *Sankhya-Yogi* (सांख्ययोगी), through reasoning and thinking, and the other one is for *Karma-Yogi*, through *Karma–Yoga*, while performing one's professional duties in this very world. Both paths lead to the attainment of *Brahm-Nirvana* (ब्रह्म निर्वाण) in stages and phases". Krishna continues to explain, "A person cannot obtain the state of Nishkam Karma by abdicating one's professional Karma and by not doing what must be done. A person with untrained mind cannot attain the *siddhi*, the state, of Brahm-Nirvana (ब्रह्म निर्वाण)." He thus implies that the mind needs to be trained in stages- *Karma, Nishkam Karma, Sthit-Pragya, Brahmi-Sthiti and, then, Brahm-Nirvana*, which is a realization of the ultimate reality through ultimate wisdom. Arjun must not skip stages, by not performing his Karma, in a hurry to attain Brahm-Nirvana (ब्रह्म निर्वाण).

As shown in Figure: 2.2, there is a one-to-one relationship between the layers of abstraction of human existence and the evolutionary stages which lead to the realization of *Brahm-Nirvana* (ब्रह्म निर्वाण). Krishna would like Arjun not to skip the first two stages of Karma and Nishkam Karma and, like a *Sankhya-Yogi*(सांख्ययोगी), enter straight into the third stage of Sthit-Pragya (स्थितप्रज्ञ). To make his point clearer, he states:

न हि कश्चित् क्षणम् अपि जातु तिष्ठति अकर्मकृत्
कार्यते हि अवशः कर्म सर्वः प्रकृतिजैः गुणैः (३-५)

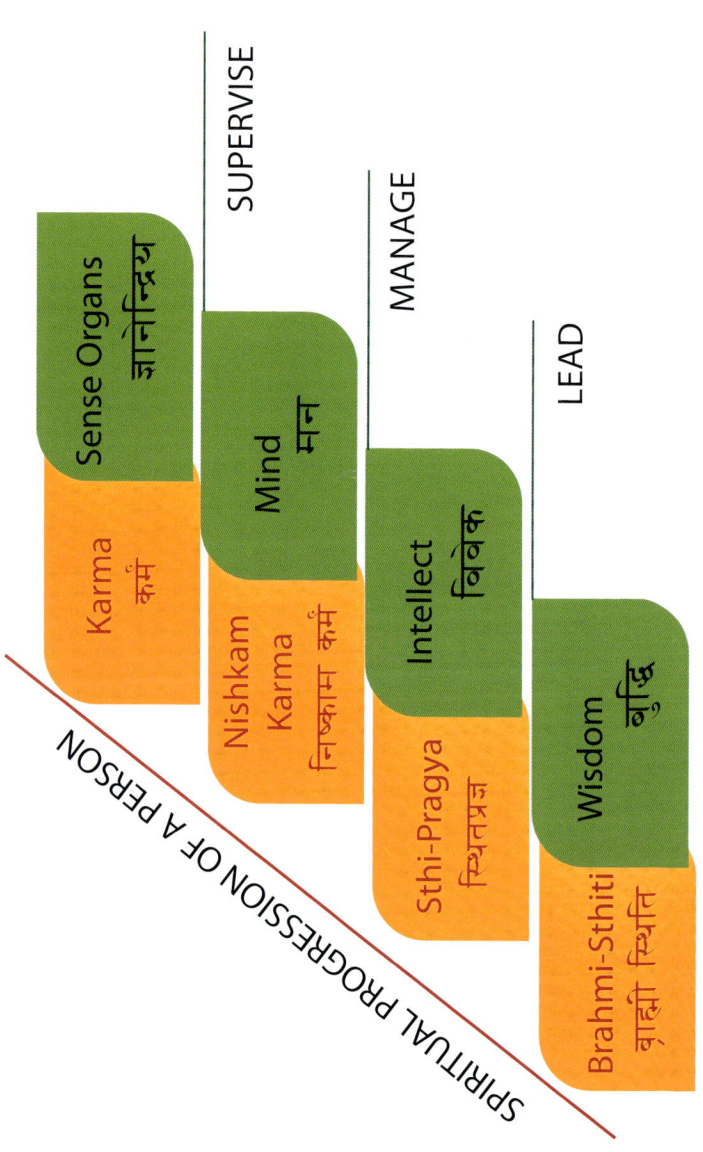

SPIRITUAL PROGRESSION OF A PERSON

SUPERVISE

Sense Organs
ज्ञानेन्द्रिय

Karma
कर्म

MANAGE

Mind
मन

Nishkam Karma
निष्काम कर्म

LEAD

Intellect
विवेक

Sthi-Pragya
स्थितप्रज्ञ

Wisdom
बुद्धि

Brahmi-Sthiti
ब्राह्मी स्थिति

Figure: 2.2 Spiritual Progression of a Person

"No one can exist without doing some Karma. Everyone in this world is impelled by forces according to one's nature to do some Karma." As one might say, Krishna was confronting a problem of his own making. He started convincing Arjun to fight in the war by taking the high road of starting with a vision of Atman. Arjun, now, wants to attain that vision in one high jump. Krishna's problem, now, is how to pull Arjun away from his desire for 'high jump to wisdom' and make him traverse the path in all its stages. He shifts his strategy gear and starts praising the virtue of performing one's professional and desirable duties. He strives to convince Arjun that those who are capable of engaging in worldly affairs with an unattached mind, with objectivity, they are truly an admirable bunch. As he says:

कर्म इन्द्रियैः कर्मयोगम् असक्तः सः विशिष्यते (३:७)

Furthermore,

नियतं कुरु कर्म त्वं ज्यायः हि अकर्मणः
शरीरयात्रा अपि च ते न प्रसिद्धेत् अकर्मणः (३:८)

"You should always do some Karma because Karma is better than *Akarma* (अकर्म); doing something is always better than not doing anything. And, even one's own livelihood is not possible with *Akarma* (अकर्म), without doing anything." What a clever leadership tactics? From being on a very high visionary pedestal with profound thoughts of 'sense organs-mind-intellect-wisdom (ज्ञानेन्द्रिय, मन, विवेक, बुद्धि)' formulation, now, Krishna has come down to the level of feeding the stomach! He seems to be exhorting Arjun, 'Not doing a Karma will lead to starvation, Arjun, get up and fight in the war.' As he has said before, "धर्मात् हि युद्धात् श्रेयः अन्यत् क्षत्रियस्य न विद्यते (२:३१), for a warrior, there is no better thing to do than going to a just and a lawful war". After coming down to the level of feeding the stomach, Krishna switches back again to a higher plane with the same felicity with which he had descended from a higher plane to a lower one. Let's see what he says now:

कर्म   ब्रह्मोद्भवं   विद्धिब्रह्म   अक्षर   समुद्भवम्
तस्मात्   सर्वगतम्   ब्रह्म   नित्यं   यज्ञे   प्रतिष्ठितम् (३:१५)

"You should note that Karma is born of Vedas, which are, in turn, born of Brahman, implying that the acquisition of knowledge enables one to work and knowledge leads one to the ultimate reality. Therefore, you must do your Karma. By doing your Karma you would make progress towards Brahm-Nirvana (ब्रह्म निर्वाण) and you will realize the ultimate reality that there is to realize". He, however, does not appear to be fanatically attached to the idea that Karma is a must. He, in a clever way, leaves some breathing room for Arjun by saying that those who are 'completely content in their selves' (आत्मनि एव च संतुष्ट: ३:१७) do not need to take refuge of other created beings in this world and they do not gain much by performing Karma (कर्म) or they do not lose by Akarma (अकर्म). However, Krishna leads by his own example:

न   मे   पार्थ   अस्ति   कर्त्तव्यं   त्रिषु   लोकेषु   किन्चन
न   अनवाप्तम्   अवाप्तव्यम्   वर्त्त   एव   च   कर्मणि (३:२२)

"Look at me, Arjun, there is nothing much I should engage in Karma for, still I am performing my Karma". In this world, there is nothing he desires to obtain, still he is trying to inspire Arjun by giving his own example. He is still not satisfied and, therefore, makes another point to Arjun as follows:

प्रकृते: क्रियमाणानि गुणै: कर्मणि सर्वश:
अहङ्कार विमूढ आत्मा कर्ता अहम् इति मन्यते (३:२७)

अथ च,
तत्ववित् तु महाबाहो गुण कर्म विभागयो:
गुणा: गुणेषु वर्तन्ते इति मत्वा न सज्जते (३:२८)

"All Karma, in this world, is transpired by different aspects of Nature. However, those who have high ego and who arrogate to themselves the doer-ship of a Karma, are really being unwise. They are really not the cause and they really do not have the true knowledge." On the other hand, "Arjun, those who understand that Atman is beyond Karma and beyond that which transpires the Karma, they do not arrogate to themselves the qualities of doer-ship. Atman is objectively unattached from the sense organs and their objects." Here, Krishna is trying to distinguish between the doer of deeds, performer of Karma, and Atman. Ultimately, Krishna commands Arjun to fight in the war by asking him to engage in his Karma, in Krishna's name, without desire, without attachment and without remorse. He says, "युद्धस्व विगतज्वर: (३:३०)", fight without remorse.

As one can see, in his response to Arjun's second question, Krishna has approached the issue from various angles - Karma is better than Akarma; Atman does not get sullied either by Karma or by its causes; performing one's Karma, professionally, is a precursor to wisdom. Nishkam Karma is a major milestone which must be reached on the path to wisdom and attainment of Brahm-Nirvana (ब्रह्म निर्वाण). In the bazaar economy of modern times, with multiplicity of baskets and goods and services, the question arises as to how does a person relate to all this? One possible way to relate to all these is as follows: everyone needs to prepare themselves, with knowledge, so that they can have a basket and a place, for their basket of goods and services, in the marketplace. While in the marketplace, the bazaar, all professional duties should be done with a detached, objective mind. Continued practice of this detached objectivity will lead one to a state of *Nishkam Karma* and prepare one for further exploration of 'The Spirit of One'.

The question arises as to how one attains a state of *Nishkam Karma* in the midst of all the hustle and bustle, all the seductive goods and services in the bazaar? And, why are many people impelled to fall in the trap of doing things which should be avoided in the path of spiritual experience? Why and how do people get attached and lose their objectivity? This is the crux of the next topic of Arjun-Krishna dialogue.

Chapter III
The Third Question of Arjun

अर्जुनस्य तृतीयः प्रश्नः

अथ केन प्रयुक्तः अयं पापम् चरति पुरुषः
अनिच्छन् अपि वार्ष्णेय बलात् इव नियोजितः (३:३६)

In the context of the second question, Arjun had asked Krishna, "तत् एकम् वद निश्चित्य येन श्रेयः अहम् आप्नुयाम् (३:२), Tell me the one, with certainty, which is really a good thing to do? Should I be unattached to, unmoved by, unaffected from all the injustices meted out to us by the Kauravas or should I go to war?" It appears that Arjun, at least temporarily, is satisfied with Krishna's response to his request, "Tell me the one, with certainty, which is really a good thing to do?" He also appears to know what needs to be done. It also appears that Arjun is now more curious to know as to why he landed up in a predicament just before the war was about to begin. This is the background of the third question where he asks, "Who/what transpires to make a person unwillingly and, perhaps, unwittingly do things which should not be normally done?" Krishna's answer starts with:

काम एष क्रोध एष रजोगुण समुद्भवः
महाशनः महापाप्मा विद्धि एनम् इह वैरिणम् (३:३७)

Desire, *kam* (काम), which is born of the acquisitive aspect (रजो गुण) of the nature of a person and which is a very powerful force, is the main enemy of a person. Desire gives rise to anger (क्रोध) when it remains in an insatiate state". Desire and desire's evolutes are the reason, according to Krishna, for a person to do things which should not be done. *kam* is the connecting link between sense organs and sense objects and, upon being transpired by *kam*, a person is propelled to do a *Karma* which is not prescribed by professionalism. Anger (क्रोध) is an externally visible manifestation of *kam* when sense organs cannot attain their objects of desire. While *kam* is born of the acquisitive aspects (रजो गुण) of the nature of a person, anger (क्रोध) is born of the aggressive, 'go/no go' limbic aspects (तमो गुण:) of nature. The acquisitive aspect, the *rajas* aspect, is what is called ego in modern times and the aggressive, limbic aspect, the *tamas* aspect, is what is referred to as the id in modern times. A question arises whether *kam* becomes satiate and contented forever after a particular sense object is achieved or not. Krishna's answer to this is a definite 'no': महाशनः महापाप्मा विद्धि एनम् इह वैरिणम् (३:३७). He qualifies *kam* by calling it a *mahashan* (महाशनः), that which never gets satisfied and contented, literally, meaning that which 'eats/consumes' a lot. He also cautions Arjun that *kam* is महापाप्मा, a very powerful, impelling force which is not easily overcome. It is worth reproducing Figure: 1.1 from Chapter-I:

As is shown in Figure: 3.1, anger (क्रोध) is a consequence of desire (काम) when a desire is not fulfilled and, subsequently, when not managed well, it, eventually, leads to a person's self-destruction. Krishna, furthermore, throws light on how knowledge (ज्ञान) can be masked by *Kam*:

धूमेन आव्रियते वह्निः यथा आदर्शः मलेन च
यथा उल्बेन आवृतः गर्भः तथा तेन इदम् आवृतम् (३:३८)

The way fire gets masked with smoke; the way a mirror is covered with dust and the way placenta covers an embryo, similarly, a person's knowledge can be masked by

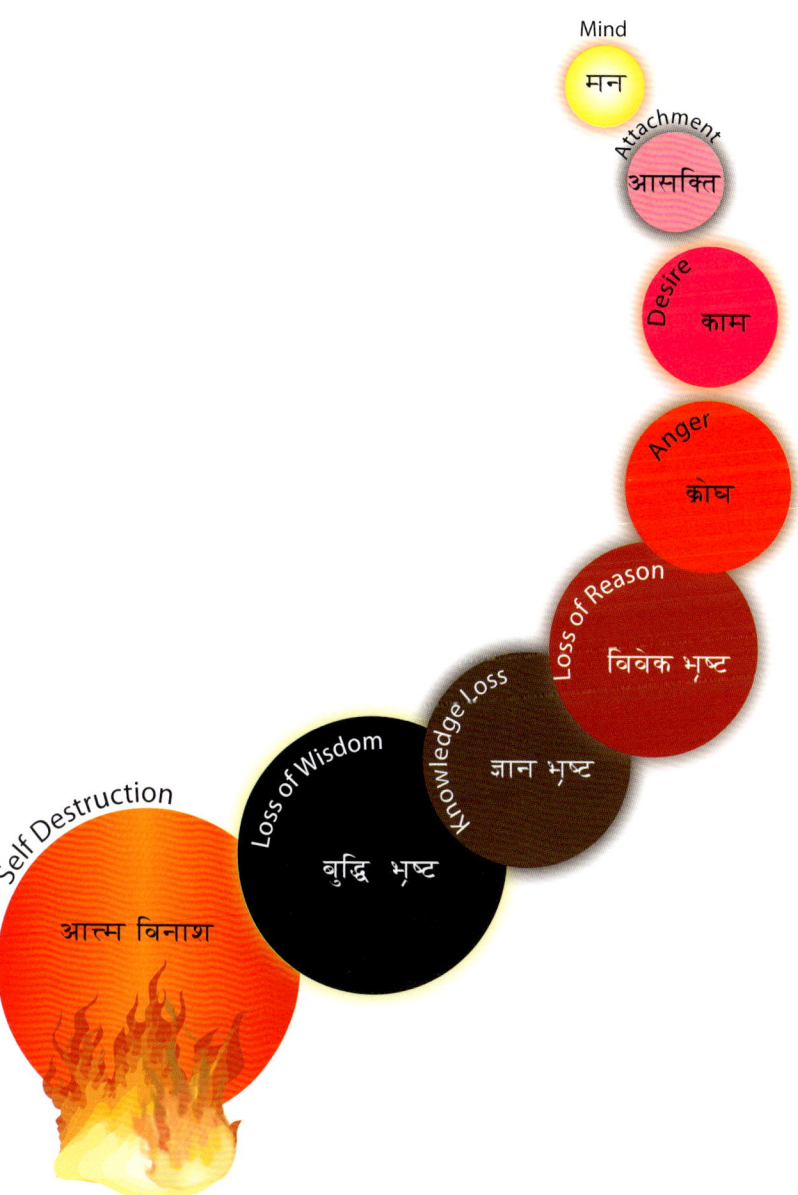

Figure 3.1

desire. Smoke, dust and placenta prevent fire, mirror and an embryo, respectively, from expressing their natural qualities of visible light, image reflection and limb movement respectively. Likewise, desire (काम), in its most overpowering state, takes away the wisdom of a person. When that happens, the worldly context assumes the qualities of inanimate beings (जड़वत). Krishna further strengthens his viewpoint by saying, 'आवृतम् ज्ञानम् एतेन ज्ञानिनः नित्यवैरिणा, कामरूपेण कौन्तेय दुष्पूरेण अनलेन च (३:३९)', this knowledge, this wisdom, is covered on all sides by 'difficult to satisfy' desire(काम), which is like a wild fire that is very hard to extinguish. *Kam* is, thus, the real enemy which propels a person to do things which, otherwise, should not and must not be done. In *Shrimad-Bhagavat*, it has been similarly emphasized:

न जातु कामः कामानाम् उपभोगेन शाम्यति
हविषा कृष्णवर्त्मा इव भूय एव अभिवर्द्धते (९:१९:१४)

Desire gives birth to more desire and it does not lessen or eliminate the need to have more desires. This is, somewhat, like pouring purified butter (घी) in fire, which makes the fire even stronger. A question arises: where does this desire come from? Where is its source? If one could locate the source of this all powerful desire (काम), then, it might be possible to win over it. 'इन्द्रियाणि मनः बुद्धिः अस्य अधिष्ठानम् उच्यते (३:४०)' . Krishna holds all the four layers- the sense organs, the mind, the intellect and the wisdom- responsible. In its simplest origin, desire arises from a temporal and spatial proximity of the sense organs and their objects and due to the failure of the supervisor(the mind), the manager(the intellect) and the leader (the wisdom). This is a sort of a total failure of the whole 'chain of command' as shown in Figure 2.1 in

Chapter-II. He exhorts Arjun by saying, 'पाप्मानं प्रजहि हि एनम् ज्ञान विज्ञान नाशनम् (३:४१)', "O Arjun, therefore, destroy *kam* which is the very incarnation of *pap* (पाप्मान), and which is also the destroyer of knowledge (ज्ञान) and science (विज्ञान)." *Pap* is an unprofessional behaviour in modern terms. How does one go about destroying the 'most wanted' enemy of a person, then? To shed light on this issue, Krishna refers to the three layers of supervision, management and leadership as shown in Figure 2.1 in Chapter-II. However, he adds one more layer, which is beyond wisdom (बुद्धि), as shown in Figure 3.2:

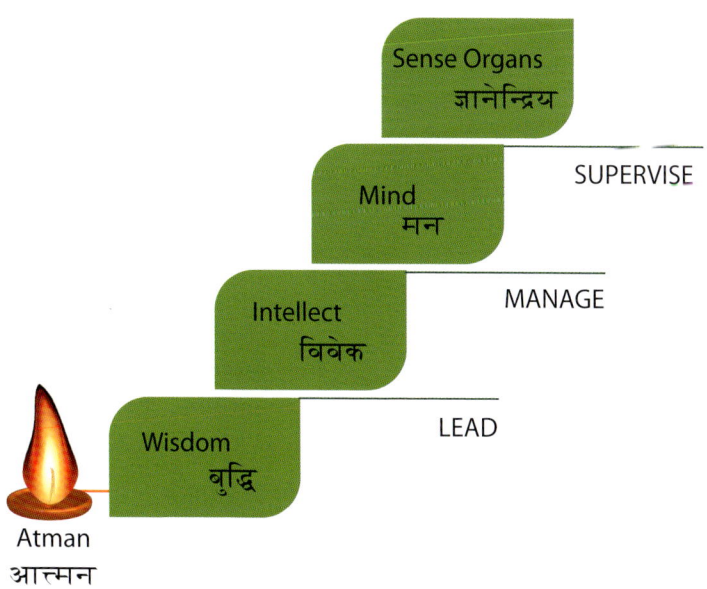

Figure 3.2

As he puts it, बुद्धेः यः परः तु सः (३:४२)', *that which is beyond wisdom is the very Atman.* Thus, in response to Arjun's third question, 'Who/what transpires to make a person unwillingly do things which should not be normally done?', Krishna firmly establishes that it is the desire, *kam*, which is the all powerful force and which must be overcome to prevent a person from doing things which should not and must not be normally done. He also extends the model of 'sense organs, mind, intellect and wisdom' to one more layer to include *Atman* so that a process can be found to achieve the objective of winning *kam* over and perform one's duties in the most professional way through the principle of *Nishkam Karma*. Krishna's answer, which starts with 'काम एष क्रोध एष रजोगुण समुद्भवः महाशनः महापाप्मा विद्धि एनम् इह वैरिणम् (३:३७)' this desire, *kam* (काम), which is born of an acquisitive aspect (रजो गुण) of the nature of a person and which is a very powerful force, is the main enemy of a person. Desire gives rise to anger (क्रोध) when it remains in an insatiate state' and ends with 'पाप्मानं प्रजहि हि एनम् ज्ञान विज्ञान नाशनम् (३:४१)', 'Arjun, therefore, destroy this very incarnation of *pap* (पाप्मान), the *kam*, which is the destroyer of knowledge (ज्ञान) and science (विज्ञान)'. Krishna also tells Arjun that this knowledge is very ancient in its origin and this is what he had shared with the Sun (सूर्य) who, in turn, had shared this with Manu (मनु) and who, in turn, shared with Ikshvaku (इक्ष्वाकु). He is implying that he is doing his duty, again, by sharing this cross-generational knowledge with Arjun in this new time and age and that an understanding of the five-layer model of a human being, as shown in Figure 3.2, is an essential step towards achieving *Nirvana*.

It is worth noting that Krishna, here, implies that he was also there at the time of the Sun. Is he alluding to a temporal transcendence? He already has introduced the concept of Atman in the spiritual model and he appears ready to introduce another concept of *Akal or kutastha*, temporal transcendence as he attempts to respond to the fourth question of Arjun. This is a key concept which will help one to keep one's head above the water in the complex maze of the bazaar economy.

Chapter IV
The Fourth Question of Arjun

अर्जुनस्य चतुर्थः प्रश्नः

Krishna had opened another door for Arjun to ask his fourth question by stating, earlier, that it was he who had shared the knowledge of *Karma Yoga* (कर्मयोग) with the Sun (सूर्य) in ancient times. Arjun asks,

अपरं भवतो जन्म परं जन्म विवस्वतः
कथं एतत् विजानीयां त्वम् आदौ प्रोक्तवान् इति (४:४)

"You have been born in our times and you are my peer, why should I believe that it was you who shared this knowledge with the Sun in ancient times (४:४)?" In other words, Arjun is demanding a convincing proof for Krishna's claim that he has been around since the beginning of time; the Sun being a metaphor for time. Well, after introducing the concept of *Atman* and its indestructibility, it should not be difficult to go to the next logical plane. Or should it be? Krishna is also a person who has realized *Brahman* and, therefore, from now onwards, he is making statements in a way which suggests his identity with *Brahman*, i.e., in a way which is, in later times, akin to Jesus' *kabalistically* inspired, spiritual exclamation of 'The Father and I are One'. In Krishna's case, *Atman* and *Brahman* have become one, *khodi* and *khoda* have dissolved into one. To begin with a response to the fourth question, Krishna makes a simple stipulation:

बहूनि मे व्यतितानि जन्मानि तव च अर्जुन
तानि अहं वेद सर्वाणि न त्वं वेत्थ परम् तप (५:५)

"Arjun, you and I have been born several times in the past. However, you do not know this (न त्वं वेत्थ) but I have a memory of all those times (तानि अहं वेद सर्वाणि) when we were born in the past." How is it possible for anyone to remember 'cross-life' experiences? If it is possible for Krishna to remember, then, why is it not possible for Arjun? What is the difference? Is there a difference in the way Krishna gets born and the way Arjun and other human beings and other life forms get born? This is the crux of this question. Let's see what Krishna says:

अजः अपि सन् अव्यय आत्मा भूतानाम् ईश्वरः अपि सन्
प्रकृतिं स्वाम् अधिष्ठाय सम्भवामि आत्ममायया (८:६)

Even though I am unborn (अज), indestructible (अव्यय आत्मा) and *Ishvar* (ईश्वर) for all beings, I assume this gross body form with the help of my own consciousness (आत्ममाया) and the 'animate aspect of my own inherent energy' (चितशक्ति). Question arises as to what is that consciousness which Arjun does not possess? What is the difference in what Krishna has described himself to be and what an ordinary person like Arjun is? If Krishna's *Atman* is indestructible, so is everyone else's Atman, too. He already has said exactly that when he was laying down the vision of *Atman*. That vision does not apply to only his *Atman*; it applies to everyone else's, too. If he is unborn (अज), so is everyone else, too, by the virtue of everyone else's subtle 'body' (देह) acquiring the gross body form (देही) again after the existing gross body form (देही) passes away. So if something never 'died' in the first place anyway, therefore, that thing is never born or is 'always born' in the sense Krishna describes himself to be. So how does Krishna have a memory of what happened in times, long past, and Arjun does not?

There is a subtle difference. That difference is rooted in the different kinds of 'unborn-ness' (अजत्व) of an ordinary being, whose *Atman*, due to a lack of understanding, is closely 'tied' to the gross body form and that of Krishna, whose *Atman* is not closely 'tied' to the gross body form. Since he understands the true nature of things, his 'unborn-ness' (अजत्व) and 'born-ness' (जन्मतत्त्व) are separate from his *Atman*. Birth of ordinary beings, in different life forms (योनि), depends upon the evolutes of their *Karma* and to what degree they were attached to those evolutes of their *Karma*. Krishna's *Atman* has reached a stage which cannot be affected by the evolutes of his *Karma* and he has attained what can be called 'freedom from affection by *Karma* or its evolutes'. Despite being 'free from affection by *Karma*', he still gets born. But his birth is of a different kind than that of Arjun and, therefore, his 'unborn-ness' (अजत्व) is also of a different nature.

The fundamental difference between the way Krishna gets reborn and other beings, like Arjun, get reborn is that Krishna's birth is due to the 'animate aspect of his own inherent energy' (चितशक्ति) and under the guidance of his own consciousness (आत्ममाया), while the birth of an ordinary being is due to Krishna's consciousness (परात्ममाया). And, the different life forms (योनि) are due to the evolutes of an individual's *Karma*. Due to this difference, ordinary beings do not remember events of the previous life forms, whereas Krishna does. Before Arjun asks Krishna why does he have to get born in a gross body form, after attaining temporal transcendence, Krishna already has lined up his answer:

यदा यदा हि धर्मस्य ग्लानिः भवति भारत
अभ्युत्थानम् अधर्मस्य तदा आत्मानम् सृजामि अहम् (८:७)

"Arjun, whenever there is a decay of *Dharma* (धर्म) and rise in *Adharma* (अधर्म), then, I take up this gross body form (आत्मानम् सृजामि अहम्)", out of my own volition (स्वेच्छया) and due to the 'animate aspect of my own inherent energy' (चितशक्ति) under the guidance of my own consciousness (आत्ममाया) as he has stated earlier. He adds further:

परित्राणाय साधूनाम् विनाशाय च दुष्कृताम्
धर्म संस्थापन अर्थाय सम्भवामि युगे युगे (८:८)

"I get 'reborn' again and again in every *Yuga* (युग) to re-establish the reign of *Dharma* (धर्म)". It is worth noting that Krishna is indicating that he takes up the gross body form in every *Yuga*. As a side note, there are four *Yugas*- *Satya Yuga* (सत्ययुग), *Treta Yuga* (त्रेतायुग), *Dwapar Yuga* (द्वापरयुग) and *Kali Yuga* (कलियुग) which, taken together, are equal to 4,320,000 solar years- 4.32 million solar years. As a reference, 4.32 billion solar years form one day of *Brahma* (ब्रह्मा) and 360 such days form one year of *Brahma* whose 'life span' is 100 such years! We are currently in the 27th cycle of these four *Yugas* and we are currently in *Kali Yuga* after which the cycle will repeat itself, starting with *Satya Yuga* (सत्ययुग). Thus, around 11.5 billion(4.32 million x 26 + 3 *Yugas* + part of *Kali Yuga*) years have passed so far. So, Krishna has already been reborn 107 (=26x4+3) times and when he takes up this body form, again, in the current *Yuga*, it will be 108th times since the beginning of the universe, which is approximately 11.5 billion years old according to Indu view. This may be one possible reason why the number 108 is highly regarded by Indu people.

Krishna is, thus, saying that he remembers everything from those 107 previous births. He further continues to explain how this is possible. He states that, 'जन्म

कर्म च मे दिव्यं एवम् यः वेत्ति तत्त्वतः, त्यक्त्वा देहम् पुनः जन्म न एति माम् एति सः अर्जुनः (८:९), 'my birth and *Karma* are of *Divya* (दिव्य) origin', which is also called *Aprakrit* (अप्राकृत) origin, implying that ordinary people are born of the *Prakrit* (प्राकृत) origin as shown, to the left of the dotted vertical line, in Figure: 4.1.

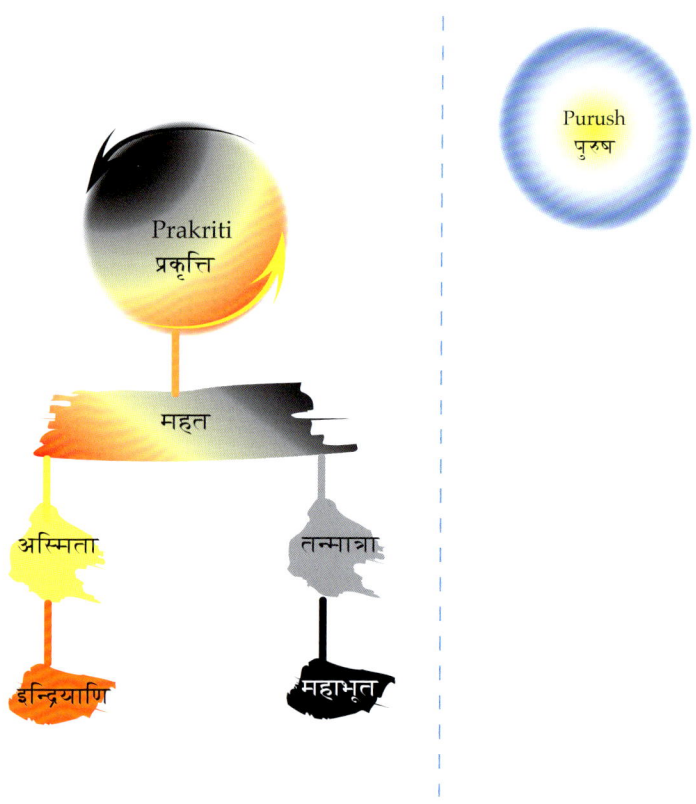

Figure 4.1

The key differentiator, thus, between Krishna's way of getting reborn and that of Arjun's lies in the fact that Krishna gets reborn under his own consciouness and out of his own volition without traversing the path shown on the left hand side branch of Figure 4.1. On the other hand, Arjun and other beings are born with the union of the *Purush Tatva* with the *Prakriti Tatva* in a complete framework of the left hand side branch of Figure 4.1. Krishna is a 'special' kind of *Purush* in the sense that *Purush* does not get tied with the *Bandhan* (बन्धन) of *Prakriti* (प्रकृति); *Prakriti's* rules do not apply to *Purush* and they do not 'bind' it. Patanjali (पतञ्जलि), in his *Yoga Sutra*, a treatise on *Yoga*, defines this 'special' *Purush* in this way:

क्लेश कर्म विपाक आशयैः अपरामृष्टः पुरुषविशेषः ईश्वरः (१:२४)

That special *Purush* who is 'untouched (अपरामृष्ट)' by *Klesha* (क्लेश), *Karma* (कर्म), *Vipak* (विपाक) and *Ashaya* (आशय) is called *Ishvar* (ईश्वर). All these- *Klesha, Karma, Vipak* and *Ashaya*- are related to the left hand side branch in Figure 4.1.

Klesha is classified, as shown in Figure 4.2, into five types and *Karma, Vipak* and *Ashaya* are related to each other in a way that *Vipak* is the evolute (परिणाम) of *Karma* and *Ashaya* is the evolute (परिणाम) of *Vipak* as shown in Figure 4.3. *Avidya* (अविद्या) *Klesha* leads a person to mistakenly perceive one thing for another, i.e., ignorance; *Asmita* (अस्मिता) leads one to identify *Chit* (चित्त) with *Purush*, i.e., ego; *Raga* (राग) is the attachment to sense objects, i.e., love, affection; *Dwesh* (द्वेष) is the attempt to get away from the objects causing pain, i.e., dislike and *Abhinivesh* (अभिनिवेश) *Klesha* is the desire for not parting away from the gross body form, i.e., a sort of 'fear of death'. The source of all the five types of *Klesha* is the mind.

Bandhan (बन्धन) has three forms - Prakritik (प्राकृतिक), Vaikarik (वैकारिक) and Dakshina (दक्षिणा) as illustrated in Figure 4.4. Prakritik Bandhan is the identification of one's ego with the eight Tatvas: Prakriti, Mahat, Asmita and the five Tanmatra- sound, touch, form, taste, smell (शब्द, स्पर्श, रूप, रस, गन्ध) - of Figure 4.1,   whereas Vaikarik Bandhan is the attachment to objects of the sense organs. The third Bandhan, Dakshina, is the attachment to Karma, Dan-Dakshina(gifts and offerings) and attainment of coveted objects.

Figures 4.1-4.4 illustrate how Krishna is trying to respond to Arjun's fourth question. The spiritual journey for Arjun is becoming complex now! Since an ordinary human being, like Arjun, is 'bound' by the three forms of Bandhan and his mind is clouded by the five types of Klesha and his birth is caused by the union of the Purush with the Prakriti along with Mahat, Asmita and five types of Tanmatra (शब्द, स्पर्श, रूप, रस, गन्ध), he does not remember what happened in the previous births. But Krishna, himself, is altogether a different being- a 'special' Purush who does not get bound by the three forms of Bandhan, his mind is not clouded by the five types of Klesha and the eight Tatva, starting with the unexpressed (अव्यक्त) Prakriti and including Mahat, Asmita and the five Tanmatra, do not affect him. He, therefore, can remember all that which happened in his previous 106 births. And that is why he has been around since the beginning of Time and he, thus, is beyond Time and its measurement. Patanjali (पतञ्जलि), in his Yoga Sutra, states thus:

पूर्वेषाम् अपि गुरुः कालेन अनवच्छेदात् (१:२६)

That 'special' Purush is the knower of all, which preceded, and is beyond the bounds of Time (कालेन

अनवच्छेदात्). Therefore, according to Patanjali's definition of *Ishvar* (क्लेश कर्म विपाक आशयैः अपरामृष्टः पुरुषविशेषः ईश्वरः), Krishna is an *Ishvar* (ईश्वर). Not only that, it is also possible, as Krishna indicates, for ordinary beings to make progress towards that special *Purush* and become an *Ishvar* (ईश्वर). It is not a question of a blind faith. Every man and woman has potential to become Ishvar (ईश्वर). Krishna drops hints like:

वीतरागभयक्रोधाः मन्मया माम् उपाश्रिताः (४:१०)
कांक्षन्तः कर्मणां सिद्धिं यजन्त इह देवताः (४:१२)

न माम् कर्माणि लिप्यन्ति न मे कर्मफले स्पृहा
इति माम् यः अभिजानाति कर्मभिः न सः बध्यते (४:१४)

Figure 4.2

Victory over *Raga* (राग), the affection for the sense objects, fear of death or fear of separation from/loss of the objects of senses and victory over anger are essential steps towards a realization of the nature of the *Purush*, the *Atman* and, subsequently, towards a realization of the special *Purush*. He also notes that   कांक्षन्तः कर्मणां सिद्धिं यजन्त इह देवताः (८:१२)', people, in this world, worship *Devata* (देवता) for obtaining desired evolutes of their *Karma*. He, here, implies that even this *Karma* is better than not doing anything. He concludes his response to the fourth question by saying, '*Karma* does not get me attached and I do not desire and strive for the evolutes of my *Karma*', न माम् कर्माणि लिप्यन्ति न मे कर्मफले स्पृहा इति माम् यः अभिजानाति कर्मभिः न सः बध्यते (८:१४)

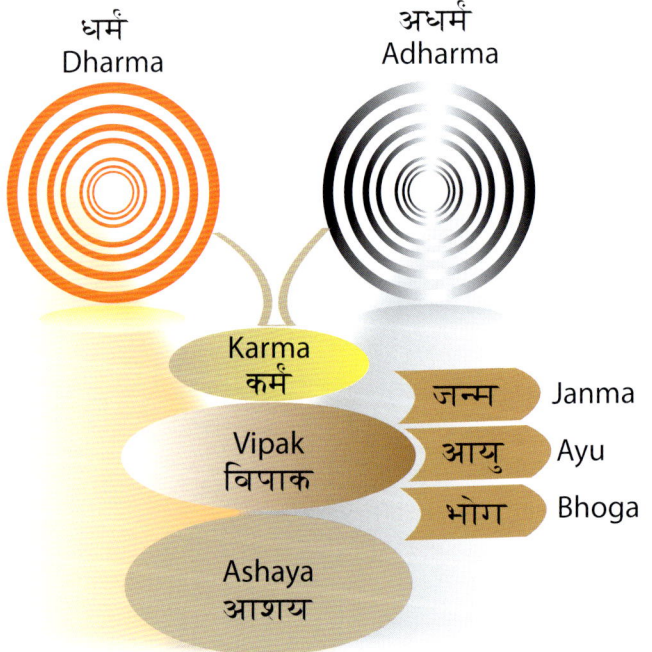

Figure 4.3

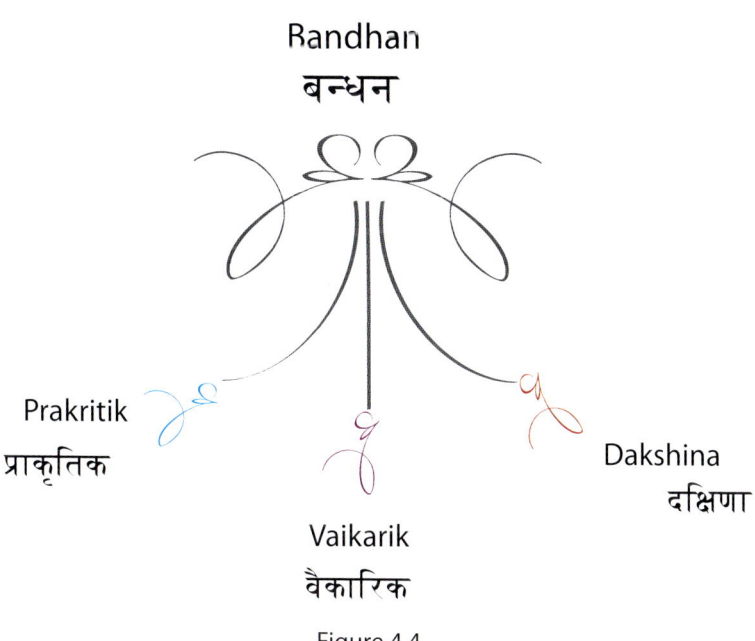

Bandhan

बन्धन

Prakritik

प्राकृतिक

Vaikarik

वैकारिक

Dakshina

दक्षिणा

Figure 4.4

Those, who know this, will not get bound by the three types of *Bandhan* of *Karma*, and thus, they will move a step closer to realizing the 'Spirit of One', their own god.

What does all this mean? In simplest terms, people should not get hung up with and attached to the physical and worldly activities, in the bazaar and outside the bazaar, they are indulging in to make a livelihood as long as they understand that they need to do something to eke out a livelihood for themselves and their family. Understanding and reinforcing this will help them to understand and reach a state of time transcendent consciousness. The idea is to live one's life with a detached objectivity so as to feel and to experience the 'Spirit of One'. This viewpoint has been taken up in the next question Arjun poses.

Chapter-V
The Fifth Question of Arjun

अर्जुनस्य पंचमः प्रश्नः

संन्यासं कर्मणां कृष्ण पुनः योगं च शंससि
यत् श्रेयः एतयोः एकं तत् मे ब्रूहि सुनिश्चितम् (५:१)

Arjun's fifth question to Krishna is: You have talked a lot about *Karma Sanyas* (कर्म संन्यास), renunciation of *Karma*, however, you are also praising *Karma Yoga* (कर्म योग). Can you tell me the one, out of these two, which is most suited for me? Actually, this apparent confusion was caused by Krishna's earlier exhortation to Arjun where he had said:

योगसंन्यस्तकर्माणं ज्ञान संछिन्न संशयम्
आत्मवन्तं न कर्माणि निबघ्नन्ति धनञ्जय (४:४१)

"O, Arjun, *Bandhan(Prakritik, Vaikarik and Dakshina* as shown in Figure 4.4 in the previous chapter) does not bind those to *Karma* and *Karma's* evolutes who have renounced *Karma* through *Karma Yoga* by adopting the process of *Sanyas*, renunciation, and, also, those who have removed all doubts and confusion through knowledge and wisdom".

Arjun does realize that as long as he is bound by the *Karma Bandhan*, as shown in Figure 5.1, above, he will not succeed in realizing the true nature of *Atman*. But, at the same time, he also does not appear to be clear about the process of getting out of *Bandhan*. Should he choose the path of *Karma Sanyas* (कर्म संन्यास)? Or, should he perform *Karma Yoga* (कर्म योग)? Which is a better process for him, he wonders. As shown in Figure 5.1, *Vipak* (विपाक) is the evolute of *Karma* (कर्म)

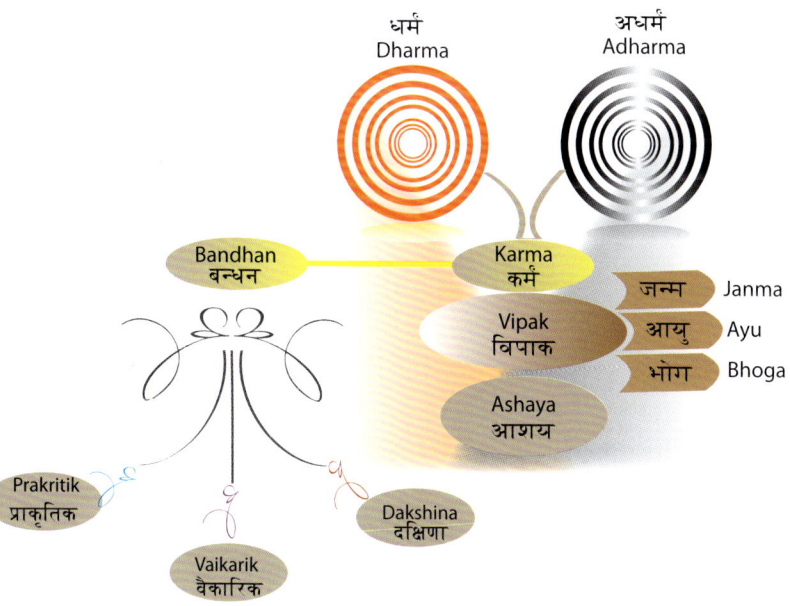

Figure 5.1

and *Ashaya* (आशय) is the evolute of *Vipak* and *Karma* 'binds' a person through three types of *Bandhan* (बन्धन), therefore, Arjun argues in his mind, 'easy way to get 'there' is just not to do any *Karma*'. When there will be no *Karma*, its evolute will not be there, which, in trun, will not have its own evolute and so on. Therefore, he concludes that a person will, thus, be closer to realizing the true nature of *Atman* and, subsequently, the true nature of the 'special' *Purush*, the *Ishvar*. It is noteworthy that Arjun had thought of this short cut earlier, too. Krishna is advising him to perform *Karma* through *Karma Yoga* and , at the same time, Arjun must do it in such a way that, while performing *Karma*, its evolutes do not 'bind' him through the three types of *Bandhan*. Well, it is a difficult task and, also, it is confusing at the same time.

Krishna's challenge is to move Arjun from the boxed areas of Figure 5.2 to the realization of the true nature of Purush, the Atman, and also, subsequently, to the realization of the true nature of the 'special' Purush, the Ishvar. This is the chart of gradual spiritual progression which Krishna has in mind for Arjun. But at the same time, Krishna wants Arjun to do *Karma* which is generally done by a person in the boxed areas of Figure 5.2. This is the source of Arjun's state of confusion and, hence, his fifth question, 'संन्यासं कर्मणां कृष्ण पुनः योगं च शंससि यत् श्रेयः एतयोः एकं तत् मे ब्रूहि सुनिश्चितम् (५:१)'. Krishna starts responding to Arjun's question by saying:

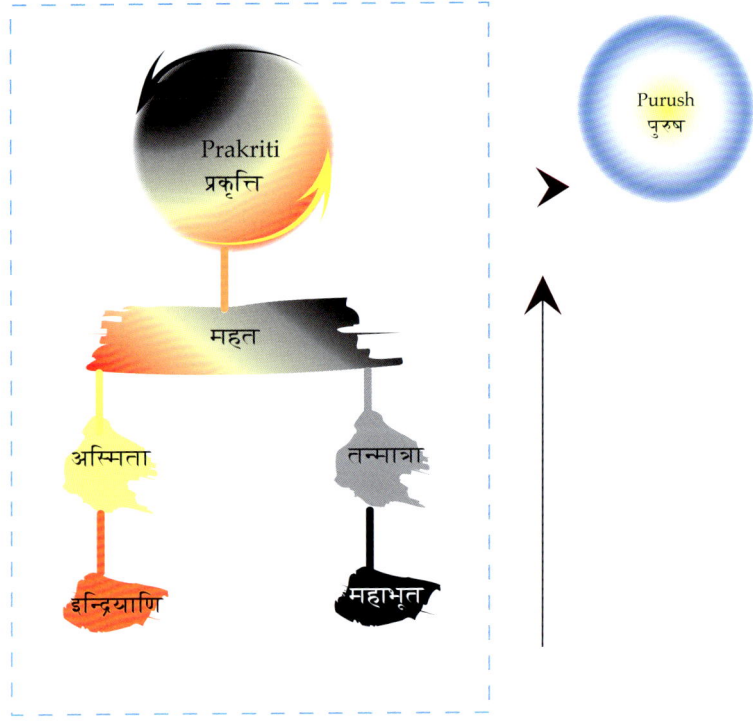

Figure 5.2

संन्यासः   कर्मयोगः   च   निःश्रेयसकरौ   उभौ
तयोः   तु   कर्मसंन्यासात्   कर्मयोगः   विशिष्यते (५ :२)

Krishna says, "*Karma Sanyas* as well as *Karma Yoga*, both, are effective processes to realize the true nature of *Atman*, however, *Karma Yoga*, when performed with a *Nishkam* state of mind, is better than *Karma Sanyas*".

Karma Sanyas is the path of knowledge, which is also called *Gyan Yoga* (ज्ञानयोग) and is also called *Sankhya Yoga*. *Karma Yoga* (कर्मयोग) is the path of performance of one's professional (क्रियमाण) duties. In Krishna's view, both of these will lead a person from the boxed areas of Figure 5.2 to the realization of the *Atman* and the *Purush*. In his response to the fifth question, he strongly hints, though, that *Karma Yoga* (कर्मयोग) is better than *Gyan Yoga* (ज्ञानयोग). It is worthwhile to point out here that Krishna has a keen interest in whether Arjun, who is one of the best warriors assembled for the war, fights in the war or not. He does realize that if he inspires Arjun towards the path of *Gyan Yoga* (ज्ञानयोग), Arjun may decide not to fight and the war will be lost without a fight. This outcome will, certainly, not be good for either of them. He further moves ahead to establish equivalence between *Gyan Yoga* and *Karma Yoga* by saying, "सांख्ययोगौ पृथक् बाला: प्रवदन्ति न पण्डिता:, only those who do not know the true nature of things think that *Gyan Yoga* and *Karma Yoga* are two different things. Those who are wise do not make a distinction between the two." Krishna thus ensures that whatever path- *Gyan Yoga* or *Karma Yoga*- Arjun will choose, since they are same in the sense of leading one to the spiritual end goal, Arjun will ultimately fight in the war. He adds further, "संन्यासः तु महाबाहो दुःखम् आप्तुम् अयोगतः, योगयुक्तः मुनिः ब्रह्म न चिरेण अधिगच्छति (५ :६), Without *Nishkam Karma Yoga*, *Karma Sanyas* or *Gyan*

Yoga is a much more difficult path. However, when *Nishkam Karma Yoga* is combined with *Gyan Yoga*, then, it leads to the realization of the true nature of *Atman* in a shorter time.

What Krishna, in a way, is saying is this, '*do your worldly duties, but do not get wrapped up in the evolutes of your actions*'. Evolutes do not have real existence; they are not real, not *Sat* (सत्). They are *Vikriti* (विकृति), a result of a transformation of something else. Whereas, *Prakriti* is not a *Vikriti* of anything, it is the *Pradhan Tatva*, the irreducible ingredient. Basically, Krishna wants Arjun to spiritually move up vertically first, and, then, move horizontally to the right, in stages, as shown earlier in Figure 5.2.

A logically consistent picture is emerging, now, in the spiritual progression of Arjun who is being led by Krishna. It is true that sense organs are physically manifest in the perceived, empirical world. The five *Tanmatra* (शब्द, स्पर्श, रूप, रस, गन्ध) - *sound, touch, form, taste, smell*- are also manifest in the perceived world. The five *Mahabhut* (आकाश, वायु,अग्नि,जल,पृथिवी) - *Sky(space), wind(motion), fire(energy), water, earth(matter)*- also extist in the physical world. For a person, it may be difficult to renounce all these in the perceived physical world and proclaim, "I do not accept the existence of all these things in this material world because everything, below *Prakriti* (प्रकृति), in Figure 5.2, is either an evolute of *Prakriti* (प्रकृति) or it is its evolute's evolute. Therefore, it does not have an independent existence of its own and, hence, it is not real, it is not Sat (सत्); it is *Asat* (असत्). Now, I, therefore, know *Atman* and also the 'special' *Purush, Ishvar*. I have discovered the ultimate Truth for myself. I am done. O, people of this world, follow me, I will help you discover your own version, your own view, of the ultimate Truth!"

However, to the contrary, Krishna is strongly advising Arjun not to turn away from the existence of the empirical world around him, but to understand it. He is asking Arjun to choose the path of *Nishkam Karma Yoga*. A question arises, then: how is it possible to see the world, to touch the world, to hear the world, to taste the world and to smell the world and to do it all with no attachment? Why are the 'impressions' of experiences of the external world so difficult to get rid of? It is all in one's head, so to speak, as Krishna says:

न एव किञ्चित् करोमि इति युक्तः मन्येत तत्त्ववित्
पश्यन् श्रृण्वन् स्पृशन् जिघ्रन् अश्नन् स्वपन् श्वसन् (५ :८)

प्रलपन् विसृजन् गृह्णन् उन्मिषन् निमिषन् अपि
इन्द्रियाणि इन्द्रियार्थेषु वर्तन्त इति धारयन् (५ :९)

A *Nishkam Karma Yogi* while performing tasks like seeing, hearing, touching, smelling, eating, going, sleeping, breathing, speaking, holding etc. thinks that sense organs and other limbs are busy doing their 'things' and, thus, that person does not consider oneself the actual 'doer' of those things. The ascription of the doer-ship for things being done is at the heart of understanding and reaching the state of *Nishkam Karma Yoga*.

The first step, therefore, is to gradually work oneself out of and above *Asmita* in Figure 5.2. As a side note, the concept of *Asmita* is not equivalent to ego and is akin to that aspect of ego which ascribes the doer-ship of actions to one's self. Rising above *Asmita* is also the most difficult step in the process of realization of the *Atman*, which is neither *Prakriti* nor *Vikriti*. *Atman* is without any evolute. It is neither a cause of anything nor an effect of anything- it is a 'non-evolute' or a 'self-evolute'. Simply speaking, it is the way it is. And the same *Atman*, when it is 'क्लेश कर्म विपाक आशयै: अपरामृष्ट:' (१:२४,Yoga Sutra), *unaffected, untouched by Klesha, Karma, Vipak and Ashaya, moves closer to the idea of the 'special' Purush, the Ishvar.* When this level of understanding for things done and the ascription of their doer-ship sets in, then, a person is well positioned on the path of realizing and experiencing a spiritual awakening.

Therefore, it is not advisable to get wrapped up in the 'doer-ship' of things. On the other hand, those who get wrapped up at the level of satisfaction of sense organs and assignment of doer-ship of actions to themselves, they are unable to move beyond the requirements of the first step in the process of realization of the true nature of *Atman* and, ultimately, of *Brahman*. As Krishna says:

युक्त: कर्मफलं त्यक्त्वा शान्तिम आप्नोति नैष्ठिकीम
अयुक्त: कामकारेण फले सक्तो निबध्यते (५:१२)

Those who perform *Nishkam Karma* (निष्काम कर्म) never get attached to the outcome of their actions, whereas, those who do *Sakam Karma* (सकाम कर्म) get attached to the outcomes of their actions and, thus, they are unable to cut the link that binds them to the three types of *Bandhan* as shown in Figure 5.3.

The 'special' *Purush*, *Ishvar*, does neither reward anyone nor does it punish anyone. The *Ishvar* does not do credit-debit accounting for people and it does not decide who will go to hell or who will go to heaven. It is through *Avidya*, ignorance, which is one of the five types of *Klesha*, that all of the life forms are 'bound' to the three types of *Bandhan* due to their inability to break the link between their *Karma* and its

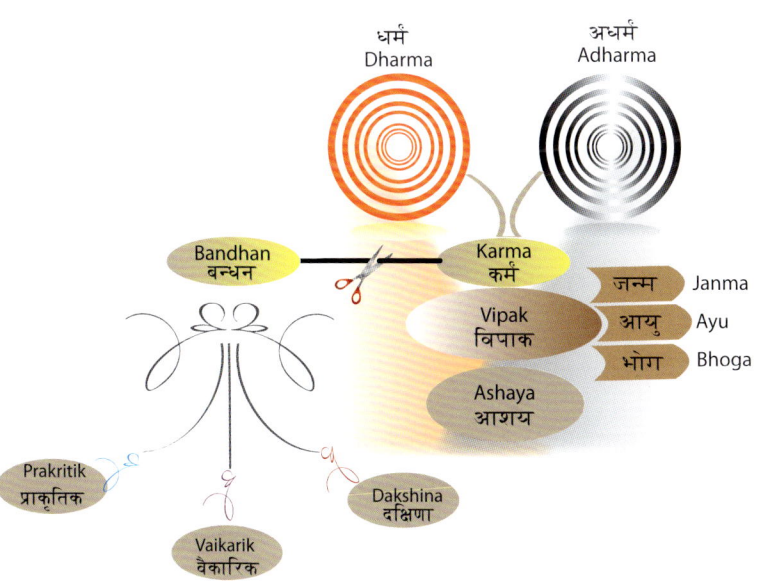

Figure 5.3

evolutes, *Vipak* and *Ashaya*, on one hand, and the three types of *Bandhan* on the other. This is also the reason why they fail to make the journey towards realization of the *Atman* and, ultimately, the 'special' *Purush* and *Brahman*. As illustrated in Figure 5.4 by the red circle, most people spend their time in this *Sansar*, this world, this *donya*, this bazaar, in an 'unrealized' state for several births and re-births. There remains a gap between their state and the state of those who have realized the true nature of *Atman* and *Brahman*.

A question arises as to how does one go about practising a process which will put one face to face with one's

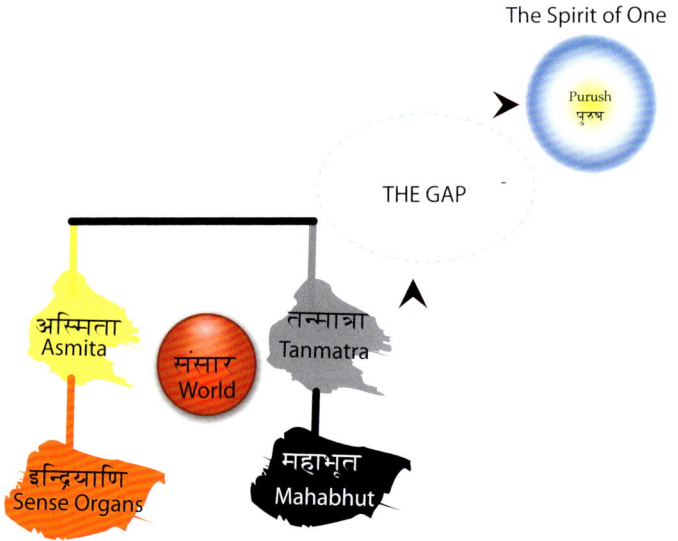

Figure 5.4

own self, first, and, then, which will lead one to experience the ultimate reality and, eventually, establish an identity with that. Mind is a good starting point as has been noted earlier. However, mind is also the most difficult subject to manage, to control and to reign in. In this context, how does one transition to a state of *Nishkam Karma*, which is an execution of one's worldly duties without attachment to them, to their evolutes and to their outcomes? This is the topic of Arjun's next question.

Chapter-VI
The Sixth Question of Arjun

अर्जुनस्य षष्ठः प्रश्नः

यः अयं योगः त्वया प्रोक्तः साम्येन मधुसूदन
एतस्य अहम् न पश्यामि चञ्चलत्वात् स्थितिं स्थिरम् (६:३३)

Arjun says, "Krishna, I understand, to a great degree, the idea behind *Nishkam Karma Yoga*. However, I am unable to internalize it due to the 'always moving' (चञ्चल) nature of the mind (मन)." He further says that 'an attempt to control the mind is as difficult as the attempt to control a strong wind', तस्य अहं निग्रहं मन्ये वायोः इव सुदुष्करम् (६: ३४). Arjun's somewhat despairing statement has a question embedded in it: "Now, more or less, I understand the ideas behind your theory of *Nishkam Karma Yoga*. How does one go about reigning in the mind?" Figure 3.2 has been reproduced as shown, below, in Figure 6.1. To recap, mind is the supervisor of all the sense organs. Therefore, logically, this should be the first place to start. On the other hand, mind is also a very powerful and a strong force to such an extent that it also has a capability to influence its own superiors- the Intellect and the Wisdom, both. Krishna, in his response, does acknowledge the power of mind.

He says, 'Undoubtably, mind is always moving around and it is, indeed, very difficult to control mind. However, with *Abhyas* (अभ्यास) and *Vairagya* (वैराग्य), it is possible to manage mind, अभ्यासेन तु कौन्तेय वैराग्येण च गृह्यते (६:३५).' Krishna offers two major tools to Arjun- *Abhyas* and *Vairagya*. Patanjali, in his *Yoga Sutra*, also confirms this view, 'अभ्यास

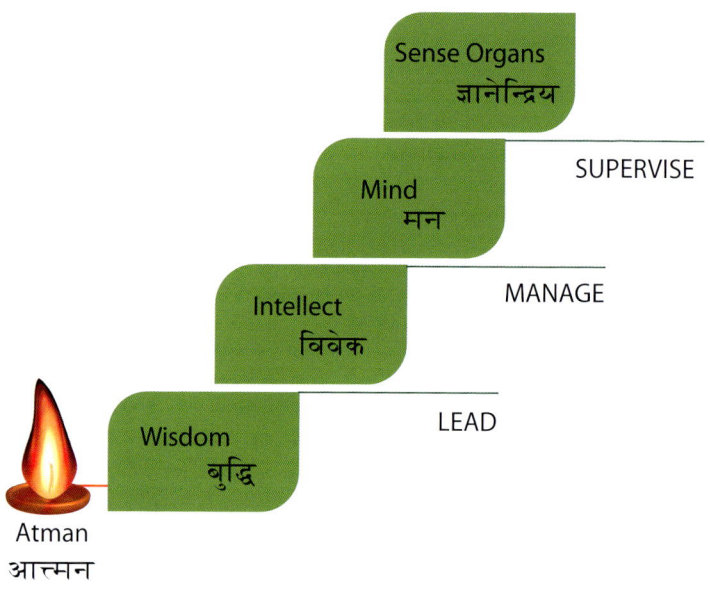

Figure 6.1

वैराग्याभ्यां तत् निरोधः' (१:१२), i.e., mind is managed through *Abhyas* (अभ्यास) and *Vairagya* (वैराग्य).

As a definition, *Abhyas* is the persistent practice of redirecting the mind to be under the control of the intellect by re-balancing the three *Vrittis* (वृत्ति) - *Satvik, Rajasik,* and *Tamasik* - of the mind. These three *Vrittis* (वृत्ति) – *satvik, rajasik and tamasik*- respectively, correspond to *Super Ego, Ego and Id* in psychology. A re-balancing of these three tendencies, *Vrittis* (वृत्ति), of the mind results in a complete banishment of the *rajasik* and *tamasik Vrittis* and *satvik vritti* becomes overwhelmingly predominant. The, mind is, thus, re-directed to 'behave' under the complete management of the Intellect (विवेक). One of the corollaries of this re-balancing and re-direction of mind's *vrittis* implies that the mind, when in the *satvik, super ego*, state, 'listens' to the intellect and whenever *rajasik, the ego, and tamasik, the id, vrittis* take over, then, it becomes difficult to control the mind.

As Patanjali states, 'स तु दीर्घकालनैरन्तर्य सत्कारसेवितो दृढभूमिः (१:१८)', *Abhyas* prepares a 'strong background' (दृढभूमि), when practised regularly with discipline, for the next step of driving *rajasik* and *tamasik vrittis* away from the mind.

Another major tool, mentioned by Krishna is *Vairagya* (वैराग्य), which is of two types: *Apar-Vairagya* (अपर -वैराग्य) and *Par-Vairagya* (पर-वैराग्य). In a very concise way, Patanjali defines these two types of *Vairagya* as follows: दृष्टानुश्रविक विषय वितृष्णस्य वशीकार संज्ञा वैराग्यम (१:१५) and तत्परं पुरुषख्यातेः गुणवैतृष्ण्यम (१:१६). *Apar-Vairagya* is a state of mind when the mind is situated in *a state of desireless-ness for worldly things and, also, for non-worldly things*. The phase of *Apar-Vairagya* extends from the start of the *Abhyas* until a 'contact' is established with the intellect. A firm establishment of a contact with the intellect is called *Sampragyat Samadhi* (सम्प्रज्ञात समाधि) as shown in Figure 6.2.

Par-Vairagya (पर-वैराग्य) is a state of mind which is attained after *Sampragyat Samadhi* (सम्प्रज्ञात समाधि) is attained and it is known as *Asampragyat Samadhi* (असम्प्रज्ञात समाधि), a firm establishment of the mind in that state. In a way, *Sampragyat Samadhi* (सम्प्रज्ञात समाधि) is the beginning of the process of relinquishing control of the sense organs, to the intellect, by the mind's two of the three vrittis- *rajasik* and *tamasik*, when mind starts listening to the 'voice of the

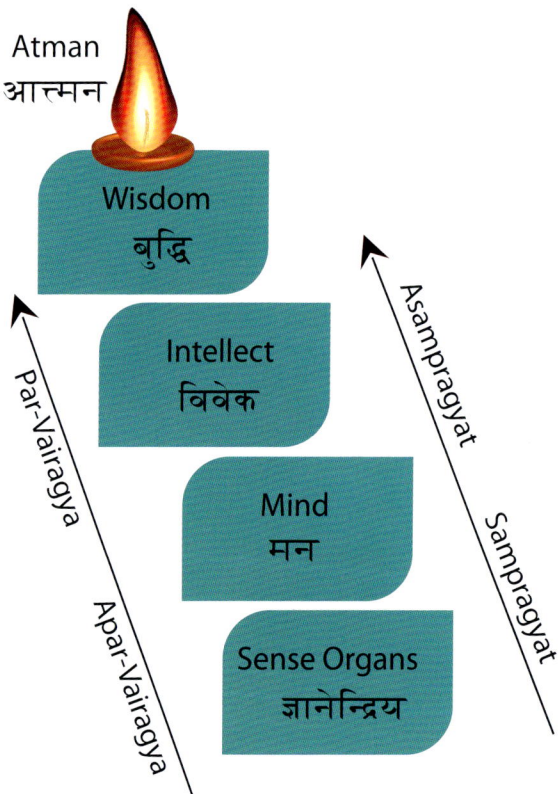

Figure 6.2

intellect'. *Asampragyat Samadhi* (असम्प्रज्ञात समाधि) is a mental state attained after the process of abdication of control of the sense organs by the mind's two *vrittis* comes to a successful conclusion. *Sampragyat Samadhi* (सम्प्रज्ञात समाधि) is the journey and *Asampragyat Samadhi* (असम्प्रज्ञात समाधि) is a major milestone, a state.

As stated before, Patanjali has defined *Sampragyat Samadhi* (सम्प्रज्ञात समाधि) as below:

दृष्टानुश्रविक विषग वितृष्णस्य वशीकार संज्ञा वैराग्यम् (१:१५)

'When the mind is situated in a state of desireless-ness (वितृष्ण) for worldly things (दृष्ट विषय) and, also, for non-worldly (आनुश्रविक विषय) things, then, such a state of mind is called *Apar-Vairagya* (अपर-वैराग्य) or *Sampragyat Samadhi* (सम्प्रज्ञात समाधि) or *Vashikar Sangya* (वशीकार संज्ञा) . There are three minor milestones, as illustrated in Figure 6.3, along the way- *Yatman Sangya* (यतमान संज्ञा), *Vyatirek Sangya* (व्यतिरेक संज्ञा) and *Ekendriya Sangya* (एकेन्द्रिय संज्ञा), before *Vashikar Sangya* (वशीकार संज्ञा) or *Sampragyat Samadhi* (सम्प्रज्ञात समाधि) is attained. A detailed discussion of these three minor milestones, which is very involved and complex, can be found in Patanjali's *Yoga Sutra*. As Krishna has noted before, 'an attempt to control the mind is as difficult as an attempt to control a strong gale', तस्य अहं निगृहं मन्ये वायोः इव सुदुष्करम् (६:३४). The most difficult part of an already difficult process is

Figure 6.3

the journey to control the two *Vrittis* of the mind - *rajasik and tamasik*. A similar thought has also been expressed in Kath-Upanishad (कठोपनिषद),

आत्मानम् रथिनम् विद्धि शरीरम् रथम् एव तु
बुद्धिम् तु सारथिम् विद्धि मनः प्रगृह्म् एव च (१:३:३)

"*Atman* is the passenger, this gross body is the chariot, wisdom is the charioteer and the mind is the rein on the powerful 'horse-like' sense organs, इन्द्रियाणि ह्यान् अभीषृन्". No wonder, then, it is very hard to control the sense organs through the application of the rein, the mind, which, itself, is very difficult to control. However, through *Abhyas* (अभ्यास) and *Vairagya* (वैराग्य), it is possible to control the mind, as Krishna asserts, अभ्यासेन तु कौन्तेय वैराग्येण च गृह्यते (६:३५).

It is important to note that the two *vrittis, rajasik and tamasik*, of the mind which need to be well managed and, perhaps, tightly controlled en route to spiritual progress, are also the creative and consumptive forces behind the bazaar economy's expansion and growth and behind provisioning of livelihood for millions of fellow human beings. How can one manage and control the *id, the tamasik,* and the *ego, the rajasik,* forces and still have a flourishing economy? If it was so difficult to control these mental forces in Arjun's times around 1478 BC and during the times before him, how difficult would it be now? Those days, there used to be, perhaps, less than twenty goods and services exchanged under the Indian *yajmani* system, but, now, there are, literally, hundreds of thousands of goods and services exchanged globally under the American bazaar economy sytem. Indeed, it is more difficult, now, to control the forces of *id* and *ego*. No wonder, then, why the chasm between the material world around us and the spiritual world within us has been widening. No wonder, then, why there were four- Krishna, Buddha, Jesus and Mohammad- titanic spiritual leaders during a span of approximately 2,000 years but, during the last 1,500 years, no one of the same stature has been born.

In the absence of spiritual titans, then, let everyone keep seeking because effort is what counts and the process of spiritual self discovery must not be given up. Having been introduced to *Abhyas* and *Vairagya*, as two major spiritual tools, Arjun continues with his seventh question.

Chapter-VII
The Seventh Question of Arjun

अर्जुनस्य सप्तमः प्रश्नः

अयतिः श्रद्धया उपेतः योगात् चलित मानसः
अप्राप्यन् योग संसिद्धिम् कां गतिं कृष्ण गच्छति (६:३७)

It has been noted in the last chapter that, through *Abhyas* (अभ्यास) and *Vairagya* (वैराग्य), it is possible to control the *vrittis* of the mind and prepare a context to move on the spiritual journey of realizing *Atman*. Krishna has asserted, अभ्यासेन तु कौन्तेय वैराग्येण च गृह्यते (६:३५).

Arjun now says, "Krishna, there are those who start on this journey of re-directing their mind, while paying a great attention to the process. For some reason, suppose, they do not complete the journey. What state do they reach after stopping on the way to *Nirvana*, the goal of *Yoga-Siddhi* (योगसिद्धि)?" In a way, Arjun is asking, "Is there something in between? Is there an intermediate degree, an intermediate certificate to show?"

He further expands on his question, "क्वचित् न उभय विभ्रष्टः छिन्न अभ्रम् इव नश्यति, अप्रतिष्ठः महबाहो विमूढः ब्रह्मणः पथि (६:३८), is it likey for a person, who started on the journey to understand the true nature of *Atman* and *Brahman* but got stuck in between the paths of *Karma Yoga* and *Gyan Yoga*, to completely waste his unfinished task?" 'एतत् मे संशयं कृष्ण', this is my doubt, Krishna, please clarify. Krishna responds,

पार्थ न एव इह न अमुत्र विनाशः तस्य विद्यते
न हि कल्याण कृत् कश्चिद् दुर्गतिम् तात गच्छति (६:४०)

Krishna's answer is a definite no. He says, "Neither in this temporal world (मनुष्य लोक) nor in that time-transcendent world (देव लोक), a person, who was on the way to do 'good things', suffers". The point Krishna is making is that those who are almost wholly engaged in satisfying their sense organs (इन्द्रिय तर्पण), devoted to the service of *id* and *ego*, *tamas* and *rajas*, and are not even trying to understand the true nature of *Atman* and *Brahman* are close to being animals in this world (विधि शून्य). Being *Vidhi Shunya* (विधि शून्य), such people are called *Avaidh* (अवैध). Therefore, en route to spiritual self discovery, trying and failing is a much better option than not trying at all. As he further says,

प्राप्य पुण्यकृतां लोकान् उषित्वा शाश्वतीः समाः
शुचीनाम् श्रीमताम् गेहे योगभ्रष्टः अभिजायते (६:४१)

Those who could not complete the process successfully get reborn in 'good' homes after spending their transitional abode among those who did good deeds while they were in this world. 'न इह अभिक्रमनाशः अस्ति (२:६०)', no amount of effort gets wasted on this path, declares Krishna. In the context of indestructibility of *Atman* as stated earlier by Krishna, such spiritual effort transcends the cycle of birth and death and threads can be picked up again in the succeeding cycles of birth and rebirth. *Sanskars* (संस्कार), impressions, of Atman are also transcendent across several rounds of the cycle of birth and death. Therefore, there is no need to worry about the outcomes of the failure in one's sincere efforts in one life-cycle.

There is another aspect to Arjun's doubt regarding the success or failure of a person's spiritual quest. This aspect raises a question as to why a person might fail? What are the impediments in the way of controlling the *vrittis* of mind and the realization of the nature of *Atman* and *Brahman*. Patanjali has enumerated the impediemnts thus:

व्याधि स्त्यान संशय प्रमाद आलस्य अविरति भ्रान्तिदर्शन अलब्धभूमिकत्व अनवस्थितत्वानि चित्तविक्षेपा: ते अन्तरांया:(१:३०)

According to Patanjali, there are nine potential impediments in the path of controlling the *vrittis* of mind. They are: *Vyadhi* (व्याधि), *Styan* (स्त्यान), *Sanshay* (संशय), *Pramad* (प्रमाद), *Alasya* (आलस्य), *Avirati* (अविरति), *Bhranti-Darshan* (भ्रान्तिदर्शन), *Alabdh-Bhumikatva* (अलब्धभूमिकत्व), *Anavasthitatva* (अनवस्थितत्व). These can be, approximately, translated into English as: *sickness, langour, doubt, insincerity, laziness, addiction, flawed perception, failure to achieve a Yogic stage and failure to hold on to an achieved Yogic stage*. It has been noted earlier that the mind has three *vrittis- satvik, rajasik and tamasik*. These *vrittis* are the three metnal states. If classified according to the 'means' of the states of mind, there are other five *vrittis*: (1) *Praman* (प्रमाण), (2) *Viparyay* (विपर्यय), (3) *Vikalp* (विकल्प), (4) *Nidra* (निद्रा) and (5) *Smriti* (स्मृति). *Praman* (प्रमाण) is the direct conduit (नलिका) between the mind and the sense objects. *Viparyay* (विपर्यय) is a flawed observation and conclusion, which is caused by one of the five types of *Klesha- Avidya* (अविद्या), which has five types of its own- *Tamas* (तमस्), *Moh* (मोह), *Maha Moh* (महामोह), *Tamisra* (तमिस्र), *Andha-Tamisra* (अन्धतमिस्र). The fourth *vritti* of mind, *Nidra* (निद्रा), makes *Tamas* (तमस्) its object of desire, whereas *Smriti* (स्मृति), the fifth one, is the impression, in the mind, of something 'experienced' before.

Another question arises, now: Are the nine obstacles (विघ्न), as described earlier, related in some ways to the five

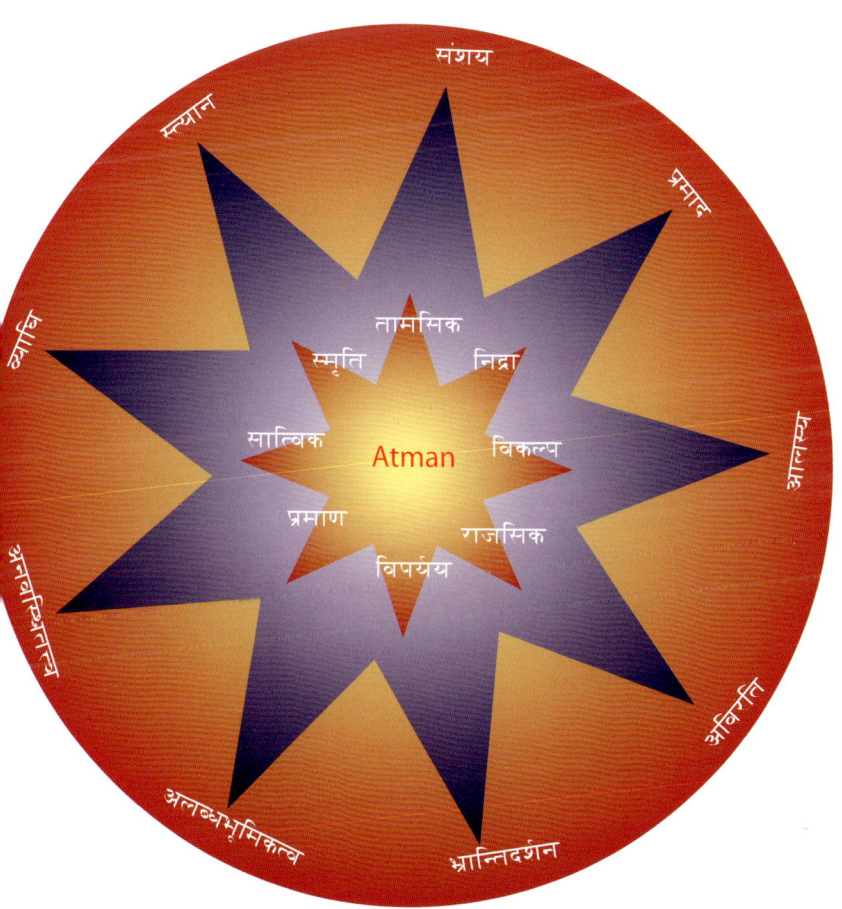

Nine Obstacles and Eight Vritis
Figure 7.1

vrittis and, thus, pose a problem in the path of realization of the nature of *Atman*? Well, *Sanshay* (संशय) and *Bhranti-Darshan* (भ्रान्तिदर्शन) are *Viparyay Vritti* itself and, therefore, when *Sanshay* (संशय) and *Bhranti-Darshan* (भ्रान्तिदर्शन) take over the mind, they give rise to the *Viparyay Vritti*. Other seven obstacles, sort of, co-habit with the *Vrittis*, because they do not have existence which is independent of the existence of the *Vrittis*. Whenever they become ascendent in mind, the *Vrittis* also become ascendent. As one can see, Arjun's fear of 'getting lost' on the way of realization of *Atman* and *Brahman* is full of potential obstacles (विघ्न), as shown in Figure 7.1.

He has to not only re-direct the *vrittis* of the mind but also face active obstacles and, therefore, he has to make double effort to achieve, first, the *Sampragyat Samadhi* (सम्प्रज्ञात समाधि) and, then, *Asampragyat Samadhi* (असम्प्रज्ञात समाधि). After attaining, completely, a state of *Asampragyat Samadhi* (असम्प्रज्ञात समाधि), where तत्परं पुरुषख्यातेः गुणवैतृष्ण्यम् (१:१६), as Patanjali has formulated, even the *satvik* state, the super ego state, is transcended and when there is a complete reign of गुणवैतृष्ण्यम् – a state of mind which transcends all the three states- *satvik, rajasik and tamasik*, a person enjoys a state of complete desireless-ness, even the desire for knowing goes away. Such a mind, at this stage of spiritual evolution, is completely ready to realize *Atman* and *Brahman*.

In case a person does not reach that state, all will not be lost as Krishna has alluded earlier. If a person gets stuck and succeeds in crossing the bounds of only the *Dakshina Bandhan*, as shown in Figure 7.2, that person will start from there in his next life-cycle. In case, he has crossed the bounds of *Vaikarik Bandhan*, he will start from there. His *Karma, Vipak* and *Ashaya* will ensure that there is a 'built-in' memory of the stage he had achieved previously. And, in case, if he succeeds

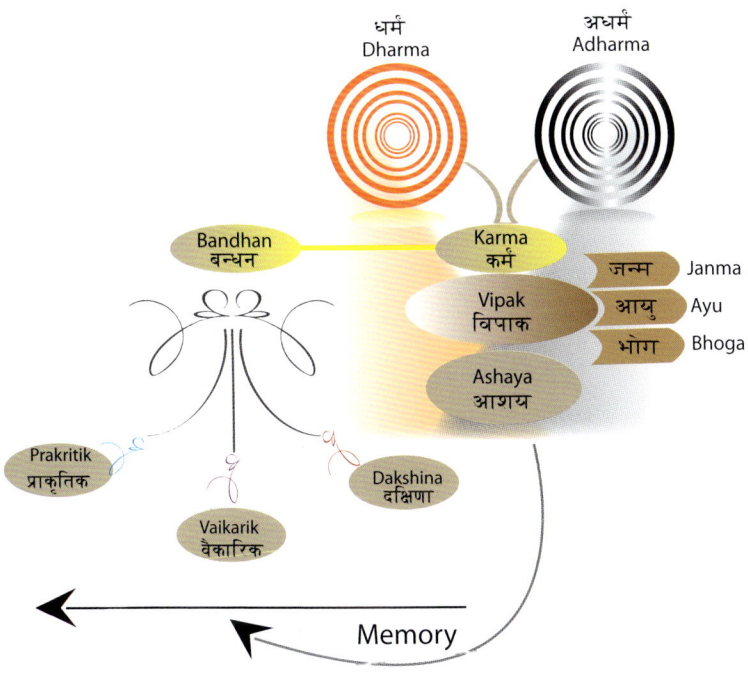

Figure 7.2

in going beyond the bounds of *Prakritik Bandhan*, he is almost there, anyway. Therefore, Krishna asserts that, प्राप्य पुण्यकृतां लोकान् उषित्वा शाश्वतीः समाः शुचीनाम् श्रीमताम् गेहे योगभ्रष्टः अभिजायते (६:४१) those who could not complete the process successfully get reborn in 'good' homes after spending their transitional abode among those who did good deeds while they were in this world. 'न इह अभिक्रमनाशः अस्ति (२:४०)', no amount of effort gets wasted on the spiritual path.

This is a very important understanding in the sense that Krishna is talking not only about the time transcendent nature of *Atman*, but also about the time transcendent nature of the process of the spiritual quest itself. When the process and the goal are both time transcendent, then, how any amount of effort could go waste? This point of view about the process, which transcends physical forms, will be very helpful in evolving an understanding of the nature of the spiritual process in our fast moving and ever changing material world of today. Is there also a piece of the external time transcendent reality in each of us, then? If yes, how do they relate to each other? This is the next topic of conversation between Arjun and Krishna.

Chapter-VIII
The Eighth Question of Arjun

अर्जुनस्य अष्टमः प्रश्नः

Arjun's spiritual curiosity has been sufficiently aroused to the extent that he appears to be receptive to learn more about the time transcendent, that which is not bound by time and that which is truly free. He asks his eighth question:

किम् तद् ब्रह्म किं अध्यात्मं किं कर्म पुरुष उत्तमः
अधिभूतम् च किं प्रोक्तम् अधिदेवम् किम् उच्यते (८:१)

After satisfying himself previously that no effort, which is invested in a spiritual quest, is wasted, Arjun asks, "Then, tell me, what is that *Brahman*, what is *Adhyatma* (किं अध्यात्मं), what is *Karma* (किं कर्म) and what are called *Adhibhut* (किं अधिभृतम्) and *Adhideva* (किं अधिदेवम्)?" Actually, Krishna had set up the background for this question, earlier, by saying, "साधिभूत अधिदैवम् मां साधियज्ञम् च ये विदुः, प्रणयकाले अपि च मां ते विदुः युक्तचेतसः (७-३०)", those who know me, along with knowing *Adhibhut*, *Adhideva* and *Adhiyagya*, they continue to know me even when they are close to the end of their life. Their knowledge does not get washed away even at the time of their death. Krishna proceeds to respond to Arjun's curiosity thus:

अक्षरं परमं ब्रह्म स्वभाव अध्यात्मम् उच्यते
भूतभाव उद्भवकरः विसर्गः कर्म संज्ञितः (८:३)

That which is indestructible (अक्षर) is called *Brahman* (ब्रह्म), which is the highest *Tatva*, which cannot be reduced any further to something different. That which resides inside a living being is called *Adhyatma* (अध्यात्म). *Visarg* (विसर्ग), which is behind birth and sustenance of this life is called *Karma* (कर्म). It is noteworthy that in the *Karma-Vipak-Ashaya* model of Figure 7.2, evolutes of *Vipak* are - Birth (जन्म), Life (आयु) and Living (भोग). And *Vipak* itself is an evolute of *Karma*. That where all these get played out is called *Visarg*, which is also called *Sansar* (संसार), in some other contexts, and which is also the *Karma Bhumi* (कर्म भूमि). Krishna further explains:

अधिभूतम् क्षरः भावः पुरुषः च अधिदैवतम्
अधियज्ञः अहम् एव अत्र देहे देहभृतां वर (८:४)

"All matter, which is 'bound' by Time and, therefore, is destructible, is called *Adhibhut* (अधिभूत), *Purush* is called *Adhideva* (अधिदेव) and I am called *Adhiyagya* (अधियज्ञ) in this body (अत्र देहे)". This is the way Krishna defines *Adhibhut*, *Adhideva* and *Adhiyagya*. Basically, Krishna is drawing attention to the model which has been conveyed in Figure 4.1 and is reproduced in Figure 8.1, for ease of reference.

Krishna's *Adhideva* is the *Purush* in the model and the emanated extension of the *Purush* which resides inside the gross body form is called the *Adhiyagya* and everything below *Prakriti* is called *Adhibhut*. The twenty three *tatvas*, below *Prakriti*, are bound by Time (काल) and, therefore, are the building blocks for the play out of this world.

Using a Persian analogy, *Adhideva* is *khoda*, *Adhiyagya* is *khodi* and *Adhibhut* is *banda*. As a side note, many may not realize this connection, but the Persian *banda* is the being who is bound by *Karma-Bandhan* as discussed in earlier chapters. The words, *band* and *bandhan*, have the

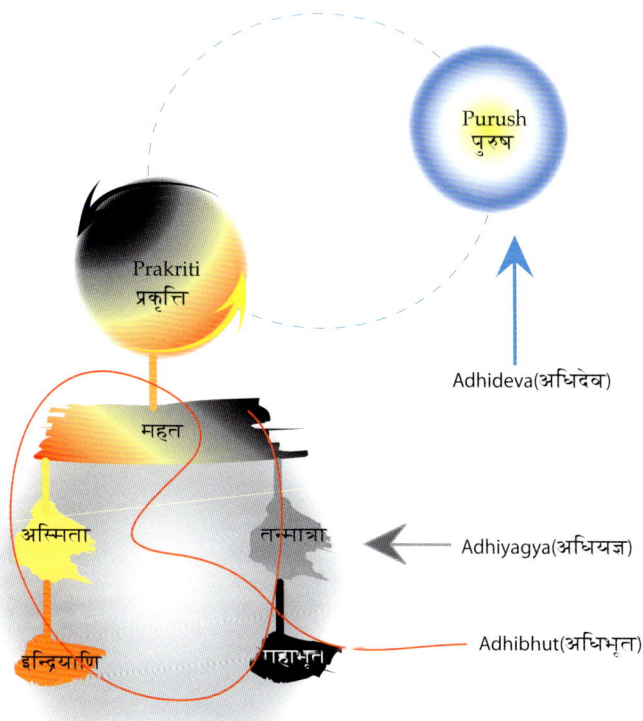

Figure 8.1

same Sanskrit root, *bandh*. Thus, as a summary, *Adhibhut* is the 'Time-Bound' (**काल-बद्ध**) expression of what is there which transcends the phenomenal world. *Adhiyagya* is the extension of that which transcends the Time-Bound phenomenal world inside every being in this phenonemal world. *Adhideva* is that which is never 'Time-Bound' (**अकाल**), which is is always there the way it is. It just "is" and it was in the past and it will be in the future. As another side note, for Akali Sikh people of India, this 'Time Un-boundedness' (**अकाल**) aspect of the Transcendent is the highest *Tatva*. They greet each other by saying *Sat Shree Akal* (सत् श्री अकाल), that 'auspicious/ beautiful one' (श्री) which is 'not bound by Time' (अकाल) is the Truth (सत्). Those who follow this philosophy are called Akali (अकाली) Sikh. As a corollary, that which is bound by Time, which includes all of this phenomenal world below *Prakriti* in Figure 8.1, is not the Truth. *Adhibhut* and *Adhiyagya* have been, metaphorically, described thus in Shwetashwatar Upanishad (श्वेताश्वतर उपनिषद),

द्वा सुपर्णा सयुजा सखाय समानं वृक्षं परिषष्वजाते
तयो: अन्य: पिप्पलं स्वाद्वत्ति अनश्नन् अन्य: अभिचाकशीति (८ :६)

"Two birds, like companions who are always united, co-habit the same tree. Of these two, one eats the sweet fruit, according to one's *Karma*, and the other looks on without eating the fruit". Philosopher S. Radhakrishnan has commented beautifully and concisely on this when he says, "Our being in time is an encounter of empirical existence and transcendent reality. The eternal in itself and the eternal in the empirical flux are companions. *The world is the meeting of that which is eternal and that which is manifested in time.* Man as an object of necessity, a content of scientific knowledge, is different from man as freedom."

The 'eternal in itself' and the 'eternal in the empirical flux' of Radhakrishnan are, respectively, the *Adhiyagya* and *Adhideva* of Krishna. *Adhiyagya's* manifestation in a *Karma-Bound* (कर्म बद्ध) and *Time-Bound* (काल बद्ध) state is called *Adhibhut*. This body is the meeting point, the tree of co-habitation, where the individuated self, *Adhibhut*, eats the 'sweet fruits' of its *Karma*, while the expression, the extension, the emanation of the 'eternal in the empirical flux' of Radhakrishnan and *Adhiyagya* of Krishna keeps on watching dispassionately inside the individuated self. Krishna is alluding that he, in the form of *Adhiyagya* inside each being, is the universal self who is watching dispassionately the other 'bird', the individuated self, which is enjoying the 'sweet fruit' of its *Karma*.

The spiritual quest, then, is a process for the individuated self to experience the time-transcendent piece, existent inside the individuated self, and, subsequently, to connect this *time-unbounded* piece to the *time-unbounded* whole of the 'eternal in the empirical flux' of Radhakrishnan. When this connection between the two time transcendent entities is established for all of mankind, then, a strong moral basis for a true non-violent (अहिंसा) world could be established. Such a moral basis was enunciated by ancient Indian sages (ऋषि-मुनि), *Ahimsa Paramo Dharmah* (अहिंसा परमो धर्म:) *non-violence is the supreme dharma.* This line of thought is still pursued by Jains of India, even today. This principle of *Ahimsa* is not limited not only to the physical destruction of a living being but it extends to include non-violence by words and by thought also. *Manasa* (मनसा), *Vachasa* (वचसा), *Karmana* (कर्मणा)- *non-violence includes non-violence through words, thoughts and deeds.* Mahatma Gandhi, during twentieth century, used the principle of Ahimsa as a cornerstone of the Indian freedom struggle. The yearning expressed in Sufi songs and Ghazals of India, Iran and Afghanistan and the *Nirguna* (निर्गुण) songs of the Gangetic plains of India is this very yearning to connect the Time-Unbounded piece, *khodi*, within each individuated being to the Time-Unbounded whole, *khoda*, of the 'eternal in the empirical flux' of Radhakrishnan. The *Sufis* use the allegory of lover and beloved, whereas the *Nirguna* songs use the allegory of a bride and the groom. Furthermore,

समाने वृक्षे पुरुषः निमग्नः अनीशया शोचति मुह्यमानः
जुष्टं यदा पश्यति अन्यं ईशं अस्य महिमानं इति वीतशोकः (८:७)

In the same Shwetashwatar Upanishad (श्वेताश्वतर उपनिषद), as quoted above, it has been said, 'in the same tree, a person who is immersed in the sorrows of the world is 'beset with *Moh*' (मुह्यमान) and grieves (शोचति) on account of his helplessness(अनीशया). When he looks at the other, the *Ish* (ईश), his sorrow goes away'. The word '*Purush*' has been used here to indicate a gender-undifferentiated person and not the *Purush* of the model in Figure 8.1.

The immersion in 'the sorrows of the world' and the grieving on account of helplessness of a being in not being able to connect the Time-Unbounded piece of the 'eternal in itself' to the Time-Unbounded whole of the 'eternal in the empirical flux' due to being 'beset with *Moh* (attachment to the idea of being a 'being')' form the rich mountain-side upon which *Sufi* saints and *Nirguna* singers have chiselled their sad songs and ghazals over several centuries. The question arises as to how does the 'dispassionate' bird co-habit the gross body form along with the bird which is enjoying the 'sweet fruits' of its *Karma*? Subsequent questions also arise: how do they not know each other, how do they become separated and become strangers? An answer to the co-habitaion question has been given in Shwetashwatar Upanishad (श्वेताश्वतर उपनिषद), (८:५) as follows:

अजाम् एकां लोहित शुक्ल कृष्णां
                बह्वीः प्रजाः सृजमानां सरूपाः
अजः हि एकः जुषमाणः अनुशेते
                जहाति एनां भुक्तभोगां अजः अन्यः

Purush and Prakriti are both unborn (अज). However, one unborn (अज), the *Purush*, 'unites' with the other unborn (अजा), the *Prakriti*, which has three attributes, *Gunas* (त्रिगुण) - *Satvik, Rajasik and Tamasik*- portrayed as red, white and black colours, respectively, in the above verse. These three *gunas* as mentioned earlier are *super ego, ego* and *id* of modern psychology *The world is an effect, an outcome, an evolute of this union of Purush and Prakriti*. Here *Purush* has been metaphorically portrayed as a male and *Prakriti* as a female. However, *Purush is neither a male nor a female* as stated earlier in Shwetashwatar Upanishad (श्वेताश्वतर उपनिषद), "त्वम् स्त्री त्वम् पुमान् असि, त्वम् कुमार उत वा कुमारी(४:३)", '*you are a woman, you are a man, you are a young man and you are a young woman.*' It is also noteworthy that a popular Indu prayer affirms the same gender un-differentiation of *Purush*, 'You are the mother and you are the father', त्वम् एव माता च पिता त्वम् एव.

A key point to be made here is that, after the world emanates from the union of *Purush-Prakriti* duo, *Purush* 'pulls back' dispassionately, जहाति एनां भुक्तभोगां अजः अन्यः. *Adhiyagya*, then, is the bird, which emanates from the *Purush*, inside the gross body form which is dispassionately observing the other bird which is enjoying the sweet fruits of its *Karma*. The pain of separation of *Adhiyagya* from *Adhideva* is the pain captured in the songs and thinking of Jalalludin Rumi, the great sufi. The same pain of separation finds expression in the *Ghazals* of Iran, Afghanistan and India; in *Nirguna* songs of the Gangetic plains of India and in the *Bhakti* songs of Mira Bai and in the two liners of Kabir, another sufi saint from India.

The challenge of first realizing and, then, connecting the *Adhiyagya* with *Adhideva* is the spiritual challenge thrown to all beings. This forms the basis of Indo-Persian Vedic-

Avesthic spiritual quest. This is also the same challenge which Krishna threw to Arjun in the Northern plains of India some three thousand and five hundred years ago. Krishna understood that if Arjun can connect the time transcendent piece, inside him, to the time transcendent whole, outside him, and detach the time transcendent piece, inside him, from his temporal existence in the phenomenal world, then, he will be ready to fight in the war with a mental state of *Nishkam Karma*.

Briefly, the spiritual challenge confronting humanity is to find their own unique path to unite *Atman* with *Brahman*, *Khodi* with *Khoda* and the *Adhiyagya* with *Adhideva*. While realizing that there is a piece of God, a piece of Allah, a piece of Brahman inside each of us is a major milestone on this path, the ultimate spiritual goal is the union the two time-transcedent realities- one inside us and the other outside us and also inside us. This is the path Krishna is leading Arjun on.

Chapter-IX
The Ninth Question of Arjun

अर्जुनस्य नवमः प्रश्नः

Arjun's interest in understanding the true nature of himself, the *Atman* and the *Brahman* has been sufficiently aroused now, therefore, he asks, "Please tell me more, in detail, about your process of *Yoga* and your *Vibhuti* (विभूतिम्) because I have not heard enough about them yet, I am not satisfied yet (तृप्तिः हि श्रृण्वतः न अस्ति मे)".

विस्तरेण आत्मनः योगं विभूतिम् च जनार्दन
भूयः कथय तृप्तिः हि श्रृण्वतः न अस्ति मे अमृतम् (१०:१८)

Here, also, the true meaning of Yoga, as a process of re-uniting the 'eternal in itself' and the 'eternal in the empirical flux' of Radhakrishnan or the *Adhiyagya* and *Adhideva* of Krishna, or 'the lover and the beloved' of sufis and the *ghazal* singers or 'the bride and the groom' of the *nirguna* singers or the khodi and khoda of Persians, becomes clearer. After Krishna had declared, 'I am the cause behind all there is in this phenomenal world and I am also the inspirer of all the subsequent evolutes', अहम् सर्वस्य प्रभवो मत्तः सर्वं प्रवर्त्तंते (१०:८), Arjun finds it intriguing. That's why he is asking Krishna to tell him again, in greater detail (विस्तरेण भूयः कथय), about the process of *Yoga* through which an understanding of *Atman* can develop and a re-unification with *Brahman* can take place. He also wants to know about myriads of evolutes through which Krishna has expressed himself. Krishna starts by declaring:

अहम् आत्मा गुडाकेश सर्वभूत आशय स्थितः
अहम् आदिः च मध्यम् च भूतानाम् अन्तः एव च (१०:२०)

"Arjun, I am the *Atman*, which is at the core of every being; I am the beginning (आदिः), the middle (मध्यम्) and the end (अन्तः) of all that there is in this phenomenal world". Here Krishna is not propounding the theory of an all powerful God who created the earth and its inhabitants and, then, went to take rest on the last day of that gargantuan effort. Or of a God who punishes or rewards its created beings in this world or in the world hereafter because they have done this sin or not done that sin or a of God who is jealous of other Gods and, therefore, forbids praying and worshipping other Gods. To the contrary, Krishna is continuing to expand upon his secular but spiritual description of the play of the *Purush-Prakriti* duo and their role in the startup, sustenance and wrapping up of this *Time-Bounded* (काल बद्ध) and *Karma-Bounded* (कर्म बद्ध) phenomenal world . As has been said in the Rigved (ऋगवेद) 10:129:6-7:

कः अद्धावेद कः इह प्रवोचत् कुतः,
आजाता कुतः इयम् विसृष्टिः
अर्वाक् देवाः अस्य विसर्जनेन,
अथ कः वेद यतः आ बभूवः

इयम् विसृष्टि यतः आबभूव,
यदि वा दधे यदि वा न
यः अस्य अध्यक्षः परमे व्योमन्,
सः अंग वेद यदि वा न वेद

Who knows the facts about creation? Who can describe it? What materials were used to create this world? Who created this? All the gods were imagined after this creation. Whence was this created, who knows? Whence did these various created beings appear, who created them or who did not create them- all this is known to only That. Or, maybe, even That does not know (सः अंग वेद यदि वा न वेद) !

By saying, ' I am the *Atman*, which is at the core of every being; I am the beginning, the middle and the end of all that there is (अहम् आदिः च मध्यम् च भूतानाम् अन्तः एव च (१०:२०)', Krishna is not claiming, that there is a God behind all this creation or beyond this creation and that is him. What he is saying is that God exists in this very creation from beginning, through the middle and till the end. One might ask: what kind of God is that? What kind of a cause of creation is that?

It appears that the special *Purush* (पुरुष विशेष), Krishna has in mind, is not like the one which is depicted in Figure 9.1a, where, after creating the phenomenal world, as shown inside the circle, the special *Purush* sits outside the circle as a judge of the deeds and misdeeds of the created beings and passes on judgements like, 'you over there are going to heaven and, by the way, you over here are going to hell'.

On the other hand, the special *Purush* (पुरुष विशेष) is more like the one as shown in Figure 9.1b by the blue color- an all permeating God in all beings who never left what has evolved in this universe. As has been noted in the Shwetashwatar Upanishad, *Purush* and *Prakriti* are both unborn (अज), however, one unborn (अज), the *Purush*, 'unites' with the other unborn (अजा), the *Prakriti*, and, after their union produces its evolutes, that *Purush* turns away in a dispassionate manner, 'अजाम् एकां लोहित शुक्ल कृष्णां बह्वीः प्रजाः सृजमानां सरूपाः अजः हि एकः जुषमाणः अनुशेते जहाति एनां भुक्तभोगाम् अजः अन्यः'. The 'eternal in the empirical flux', the *Adhideva*, shares its *Time-Unboundedness* with the 'eternal in itself', the *Adhiyagya*. However, due to *Avidya*, *Karma-Bandhan* and *Sakam Karma*, the *Adhibhut*, the temporal being, is unable to realize the connection between the temporally independent permeation, the *Adhiyagya*, in a being and the temporally independent whole, the *Adhideva*. This dis-connection produces a feeling of separation which causes the yearning for re-union with the *Adhideva*.

As requested by Arjun in the ninth question, 'please tell me more, in great detail, about your process of *Yoga* and your *Vibhuti* (विभूतिम्)', विस्तरेण आत्मनः योगं विभूतिम् च भूयः कथय, Krishna starts counting his major *Vibhutis* (विभूतिम्), his major emanations as *Adhiyagya*. He says, 'I am Vishnu (विष्णु) among the twelve Adityas (आदित्य); the Sun (सूर्य) among the shining; Marichi (मरीचि) among the different winds; the moon among the planets; the Samved (सामवेद) among the Vedas (वेद); Indra (इन्द्र) among the Devas (देव); the consciousness inside the beings; Brihaspati (बृहस्पति) among the teachers; Kartikeya (कार्तिकेय) among the military commanders; Pipal (पीपल) tree among the trees; Bhrigu (भृगु) among the Maha-Rishis and Himalaya (हिमालय) among the immovables. I am Kapil (कपिल) among the Munis; Onkar (ॐ) among the sounds; Varun (वरुण) among those who live in waters; Aryama (अर्यमा) among the ancestors and I am Prahlad (प्रह्लाद) among the Daityas (दैत्य).' He keeps on counting all the major *Vibhutis* (विभूतिम्) and summarizes, in the end, by saying:

यत् च अपि सर्वभूतानाम् बीजम् तद् अहम् अर्जुन
न तद् अस्ति विना यत् स्यात् मया भूतम् चराचरम्(१०:३९)

न अन्तः अस्ति मम दिव्यानां विभूतीनां परम् तप
एष तु उद्देशतः प्रोक्तः विभूतेः विस्तारः मया (१०:४०)

'I am also the seed of all the beings, there is nothing in this phenomenal world which is not permeated by me. Arjun, there is no end to the list of my *Vibhutis*, my emanations, I have told you about some of the major ones, though.' This

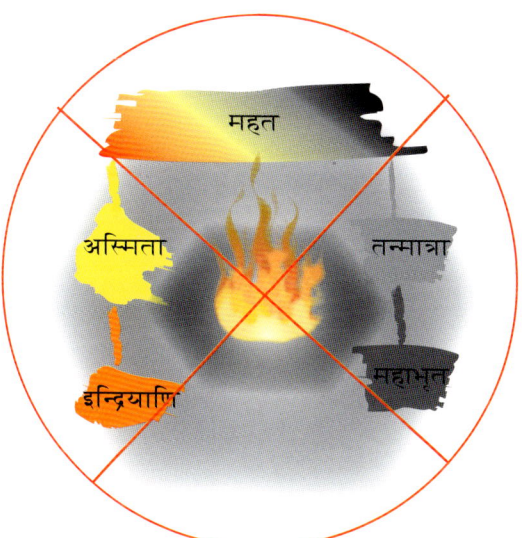

Figure 9.1a

Figure 9.1b

all pervasivenss, this omnipresence, 'न तद् अस्ति विना यत् स्यात् मया भृतम् चराचरम् (१०:३९.)' is what has been depicted in Figure 9.1b. *Abhyas* and *Vairagya*, as noted in Chapter-VII, are required to realize this permeation to establish the connection between the Atman and the Brahman. Rigved (ऋगवेद) also declares thus 10:129:4 :

कामः तत् अग्रे सम् अवर्तंत अधि मनसः रेतः
प्रथमम् यत् आसीत् सतः बन्धुम् असति निः
अविन्दन् हृदि प्रतीष्य कवयः मनीषा (१०:१२९.:८)

This is how the Vedic sage saw it, 'First, in the mind of the *Brahman*, the special *Purush*, desire (काम) was born. From that desire, firstly, the seed (रेत) of this universe was sown. The wise, searching in their hearts, through contemplation (मनीषा), understood the emanation of something which was existent (सत) from something which was non-existent (असति)'. This is very similar to what Krishna has claimed, 'यत् च अपि सर्वभूतानाम् बीजम् तद् अहम् अर्जुन न तद् अस्ति विना यत् स्यात् मया भृतम् चराचरम् (१०:३९.)', 'I am also the seed of all the beings, there is nothing in this phenomenal world which is not permeated by me'. It is important to note how the Buddhist philosophy departs from the Vedic vision. In all the philosophies, which are inspired by the Vedic thought, the 'cause' is understood to be existent for ever and, therefore, it is *Sat* (सत्), whereas in Buddhist philosophy, the 'cause' is existent only at Time "t=0" and becomes non-existent after 'what is caused' comes into being. The cause, thus, exists only momentarily. Therefore, Buddhists conclude that there is no need to invest time in dwelling on That which exists only momentarily. For this very reason, Buddhism is also called *Nastik-Vad* (नास्तिक वाद)- a philosophy based on a lack of belief in something which is

Time-Transcendent as propounded by the Vedic thought. That is also the reason why Buddha's teachings are more concerned about solving problems of what is visible and demonstrable in this very phenomenal world. Later on, after the resurgence of the Vedic thought under the leadership of philosopher Sankaracharya, Buddhist stance got somewhat diluted over the centuries. The difference in philosophies which are inspired by Vedic thought and the Buddhist philosophy has been shown in the Table-I, below.

	कारण (**Cause**)	कार्य (**Caused**)
सांख्य वाद	सत् (Existent)	सत् (Existent)
नैयायिक	सत् (Existent)	असत् (Non-Existent)
वेदान्त (Vedant)	सत् (Existent)	विवर्त (Illusory)
बौद्ध वाद (Buddhism)	असत् (Non-Existent)	सत् (Existent)

Table - I

For Budhists, Time "t=0" is not extended in both temporal directions for the 'cause' and, thus, the 'cause' does not 'need' to transcend all the three tenses- past, present and future. Since it exists at only Time "t=0", Buddhists declare that, for all practical puposes, there is no need to accept the existence of *Brahman*. For *Sankhya-Vad*, *Nyay-Vad* and *Vedant-Vad*, the 'cause', the *Brahman*, is *Sat* (सत्). For *Brahman*, Time "t=0" is extended infinitely in both temporal directions, and, thus, it exists in the present forever. Like *Sankhya-Vadis*, the Buddhists, too, believe in this time-bounded phenomenal world, which is *Sat* (सत्) in both philosophies, whereas, it is *Asat* (असत्) in *Nyay-Vad* and it is imaginary and illusory (विवर्त) in *Vedant-Vad*.

Like a commited and true *Sankhya-Vadi*, Krishna has asserted that *Adhideva* transcends Time and so does *Adhiyagya*, which is Adhideva's extension in Adhibhut, the temporally expressed being. Adhibhut is both *Time-Bounded* and *Karma-Bounded*. However, they, *Adhideva* and *Adhiyagya*, exist in all beings and they are, both, *Sat* (सत्) and are, both, unbounded by Time.

As one can see, Krishna has not responded to one part of Arjun's question- the process of *Yoga*. He still continues in his efforts to convince Arjun about existence of a time transcendent reality.

Chapter X
The Tenth Question of Arjun

अर्जुनस्य दशमः प्रश्नः

Arjun has come to a point where he is convinced that there is an element of 'something' inside him which transcends Time and, therefore, that 'something' is still there even after the destruction of the phenomenal world which exists in all the three perceived states of time- past, present and future. That 'something', as Krishna has told him, is *Adhiyagya*, the Atman, in every *Adhibhut*, in every being of this phenomenal world, which is this *Sansar* (संसार). Also, *Adhiyagya* is related to the 'special' *Purush*, the *Brahman*, in a sense that they are both Time-Transcendent.

That 'special' *Purush*, in words of Patanjali, is 'क्लेश कर्म विपाक आशयैः अपरामृष्टः' (१:२४,Yoga Sutra), unaffected and untouched by *Klesha*, *Karma*, *Vipuk* and *Ashaya*- both Time-Unbounded and Karm-Unbounded. That *Purush* is also unaffected by the five types of *Klesha*- (1)*Avidya* (अविद्या) leads a person to mistakenly perceive one thing for another; (2)*Asmita* (अस्मिता) leads one to identify Chit (चित्त) with Purush; (3) *Raga* (राग) is the affection for the sense objects; (4)*Dwesha* (द्वेष) is an attempt to get away from the objects causing pain and (5) *Abhinivesh* (अभिनिवेश) is the desire for not parting away from the gross body form- a sort of 'fear of death'. Arjun, now, understands all these concepts and he declares, 'I understand all these great things and my *Moh* (मोह) which was caused by *Avidya* (अविद्या) Klesha is gone', यत् त्वया उक्तम् वचः तेन मोहः अयम् विगतः मम (११:१).

Arjun says, in his tenth question, "O Krishna, I understand 'the way you have explained' (यथा आत्थ) to me. I have a desire to 'see' your Time-Transcedent form (द्रष्टुम् इच्छामि ते रूपम्)".

एवम् एतद् यथा आत्थ त्वम् आत्मानम् परमेश्वर
द्रष्टुम् इच्छामि ते रूपम् ईश्वरम् पुरुषोत्तम (११:३)

The way Krishna had summarized his explanation, in response to the previous question, was, विष्टभ्य अहम् इदम् कृत्स्नम् एक अंशेन स्थितः जगत् (१०:४२)', it is I who is omnipresent in all of the phenomenal world by being 'a very small part' (एक अंशेन) of it. Arjun is not sure whether it is possible for Kirshna to show him his Time-Transcedent form to his physical eyes and he expresses this fear, 'मन्यसे यदि तत् शक्यम् मया द्रष्टुम् प्रभो, योगेश्वर ततः मे त्वम् दर्शय आत्मानम् अव्ययम् (११:४)', if you think that you can do that, then, please 'show me that Time-Transcendent form' (ततः मे त्वम् दर्शय आत्मानम् अव्ययम्)', this is the way Arjun pleads with Krishna.

For a scientist, it would be easier to figure out how difficult, almost impossible, it is to visualize in four dimensions- the three spatial and the one temporal. It is even much more difficult to visualize something which is Time-Transcendent, that which is *Brahman*, the *Adhideva*, and that which is beyond the space-time dimension. This is also the reason why Arjun is skeptical and he is expressing his skepticism by saying, 'if you think that I can visualize (मन्यसे यदि तत् शक्यम् मया द्रष्टुम्)'. Krishna knows this, too, that Arjun does not have faculties to visualize beyond three dimensions, not to speak of visualizing that which is beyond four dimensions, "न तु मां शक्यसे द्रष्टुम् अनेन स्वचक्षुषा, दिव्यम् ददामि ते चक्षुः पश्य मे योगम् ईश्वरम् (११:८), O, Arjun, you cannot see that with your physical eyes, therefore, I am granting you *Divya Drishti* (दिव्यम् ददामि ते

चक्षु:), celestial eyes". *Divya Drishti* (दिव्य दृष्टि) is of *Aprakrit* (अप्राकृत) origin which does not originate from the left hand side of Figure 8.1, therefore, Arjun can use this *Divya Drishti* (दिव्य दृष्टि) to visualize that which is beyond and unbounded by space-time limitations. After receiving that *Divya Drishti*, Arjun was able to go beyond space-time dimesions and was able to visualize. What he saw, he describes in his own words thus:

दिवि सूर्य सहस्रस्य भवेत् युगपत् उत्थिता
यदि भा: सदृशी सा स्यात् भास: तस्य महात्मन: (११:१२)

He saw a burst of light equivalent to the luminosity of one thousand suns in the sky. He also saw 'all the universes' (जगत् कृत्स्नम्) expressed, in one place, in different parts of the same luminous form, 'तत्र एकस्थम् जगत् कृत्स्नम् प्रविभक्तम् अनेकधा, अपश्यत् देवदेवस्य शरीरे पाण्डव: तदा (११:१३)'. He tells Krishna about his experience thus:

पश्यामि देवान् तव देव देहे सर्वान् तथा भूत विशेष सङ्घान्
ब्रह्माणम् ईशम् कमल आसनस्थम्
ऋषीन् च सर्वान् उरगान् च दिव्यान्
अनेक बाहु उदर वक्त्र नेत्रम् पश्यामि त्वां सर्वत: अनन्तरूपम्
न अन्तम् न मध्यम् न पुन: तव आदिम् पश्यामि विश्वेश्वर विश्वरूप
किरीटिनम्गदिनम्चक्रिणम् च तेजोराशिम्सर्वत:दीप्तिम् अन्तम्
पश्यामि त्वां दु:निरीक्ष्यम् समन्तात्
दीप्त अनल अर्क द्युतिम् प्रमेयम्
त्वम् अक्षरम् परमं वेदितव्यम् त्वम् अस्य विश्वस्य परं निधानम्
त्वम् अव्यय: शाश्वत धर्म गोप्ता सनातन: त्वम् पुरुष: मत: मे

So far, Arjun has visualized in that Adhideva all the devas (देवान्), all the created beings (भूत विशेष सङ्घान्), Brahma (ब्रह्माणम्), Shiva (ईशम्) and all the thinkers and sages (ऋषीन्). He has visualized an infinite form as a source of creation (of innumerable limbs) of this physical world. Due to an infinite regression, he is unable to see the beginning (आदिम्), the middle (मध्यम्) and the end (अन्तम्) of what he saw. He feels that he has realized what needs to be realized in this world. He has crossed the limitiations imposed by the space-time based model of the universe and he has realized the indestructible *tatva* (अक्षरम्), the source of all of this cosmos (अस्य विश्वस्य परं निधानम्) and that special, time transcendent *Purush* (सनातनः पुरुषः) for whom time 't=0' is extended, infinitely, in both temporal directions. Arjun has been able to visualize what Shwetashwatar Upanishad (श्वेताश्वतर उपनिषद्) has described thus, "न तस्य कश्चित् पतिः अस्ति लोके न च ईशिताः न एव च तस्य लिंगम् । न कारणम् करणाधिप अधिपः, न च अस्य कश्चित् जनिता न च अधिपः (६:९)", of That there is no master in this universe, no ruler, nor is there any perceptible and observable quality or gender differentiation. That is the cause, the lord of the lords, of That there is neither a progenitor nor a lord. Arjun has seen That which Shwetashwatar Upanishad (श्वेताश्वतर उपनिषद्) describes, furthermore, as That which is the beginning, the source of causes which unite the *Adhiyagya* with *Adhibhut* and which is beyond the three kinds of Time(past, present and future), 'आदिः सः संयोग निमित्त हेतुः, परः त्रिकालात् अकलः अपि दृष्टः (६:५)'.

What Arjun experienced with the help of his spiritual guide and peer is the end goal of an individual's spirituality; the goal of 'The Spirit of One'. Just pointing to someone else's spiritual experience and exhorting people to blindly follow whatever has been purported to be the word of God is not enough and is not of much help. Man needs spiritual freedom instead of spiritual shackles. Despite having experienced the time transcendent reality, Arjun is curious as ever. He continues his quest as he poses his eleventh question in the next chapter.

Chapter-XI
The Eleventh Question of Arjun

अर्जुनस्य एकादशः प्रश्नः

आख्याहि मे कः भवान् उग्ररूपः नमः अस्तु ते देववर प्रसीद
विज्ञातुम् इच्छामि भवन्तं आद्यम् न हि प्रजानामि तव प्रवृतिम् (११:३१)

Arjun has experienced the form of the Adhideva,
the Brahman. He has visualized the form which extended
infinitely in both space and time and which had the luminosity
of thousand suns in the sky (दिवि सूर्य सहस्रस्य). He now says, 'I
bow before you (नमः अस्तु ते), O superior *Deva* (देववर), please
tell me some more about who you are in this 'most luminous'
form (आख्याहि मे कः भवान् उग्ररूपः), because I do not know
where will go you from here?' Arjun felt that the whole universe
was getting unbearably hot due to the brilliant light he saw
through his *Divya Drishti* (दिव्य दृष्टि). He became concerned
about the very existence of the emanant world. That's why he
asked the eleventh question, 'विज्ञातुम् इच्छामि भवन्तं आद्यम् न
हि प्रजानामि तव प्रवृतिम् (११:३१)', I want to know where will
you go from here, what will be the prognosis (प्रवृतिम्) if you
continue to display the luminosity of thousand suns? Krishna
responds thus (११:३२),

कालः अस्मि लोकक्षयकृत् प्रवृद्धः लोकान् समाहर्तुम् इह प्रवृत्तः
ऋते अपि त्वां न भविष्यन्ति सर्वे ये अवस्थिताः प्रत्यनीकेषु योधाः

'I am all destroying Time (कालः अस्मि) and I am
up to dissolving the worlds (लोकान् समाहर्तुम् इह प्रवृत्तः).
Those warriors who are lined up against you (ये अवस्थिताः प्र
त्यनीकेषु योधाः), for the war, will not survive even if you do not
kill them'. Therefore, Krishna is exhorting Arjun, 'Arjun, get

up, vanquish the enemies, earn a name and enjoy the wealth of the kingdom (भुङ्क्ष्व राज्यं समृद्धम्). All those who are lined up against you have already been killed by me(they are alive in name only), just put your signature on their death', तस्मात् त्वम् उतिष्ठ यशः लभस्व जित्वा शत्रून् भुङ्क्ष्व राज्यं समृद्धम्, मया एव एते निहिताः पूर्वम् एव निमित्तमात्रं भव सव्यसाचिन् (११:३३). Krishna further says,'Do not grieve, Arjun, you will vanquish the enemies in the war, therefore, fight', मा व्यतिष्ठ, युध्यस्व जेतासि रणे सपत्नान् (११:३४).

Arjun is now impressed and it appears that he has realized what is *Atman* and *Brahman* and he also understands the true nature of Krishna which goes beyond Krishna being his friend, his charioteer in the war and his spiritual mentor. 'अनन्त देवेश जगत् निवास त्वम् अक्षरम् सत् असत् परं यत् (११:३७)', He calls Krishna the Infinite Being (अनन्त), god of all gods (देवेश) and the source of the whole universe (जगत् निवास). He also has realized the nature of Brahman when he says, 'you are the Indestructible *Brahma Tatva*, which is beyond that which exists and beyond that which does not exist (त्वम् अक्षरम् सत् असत् परं यत्)'. At this point, the third leg of Krishna's strategy, *Bhakti-* a complete reposition of trust in the leader's ability to lead, appears to be taking over. He is almost praying Krishna as he says (११:३८ - ४४),

त्वम् आदिदेवः पुरुषः पुराणः त्वम् अस्य विश्वस्य परं निधानम्
वेत्ता असि वेद्यम् च परं च धाम त्वया ततं विश्वं अनन्त रूप
वायुः यमः अग्निः वरुणः शशाङ्कः प्रजापतिः त्वं प्रपितामहः च
नमः नमः ते अस्तु सहस्रकृत्वः पुनः च भूयः अपि नमः नमस्ते
नमः पुरस्तात् अथ पृष्ठतः ते नमः अस्तु ते सर्वतः एव सर्व
अनन्तवीर्य अमितविक्रमः त्वम् सर्वम् समाप्नोषि ततः असि सर्वः
सखा इति मत्वा यत् उक्तं हे कृष्ण हे यादव हे सखा इति

अज्ञानता महिमान तव इदं मया प्रमादात् प्रणयेन वा अपि
यत् च अवहासार्थम् असत्कृतः असि विहार शय्या आसन भोजनेषु
एकः अथवा अपि अच्युत तत् समक्षम् तत् क्षामये त्वाम् अहं प्रमेयम्
पिता असि लोकस्य चराचरस्य त्वम् अस्य पूज्यः च गुरुः गरीयान्
न त्वत्समःअस्तिअभ्यधिकः कुतः अन्यः लोकत्रये अपि अप्रतिम प्रभाव
तस्मात् प्रणम्य प्रणिधाय कायं प्रसादये त्वां अहं ईशं ईड्यम्
पिता इव पुत्रस्य सखा इव सख्युः प्रियः प्रियायाः अर्हसि देव सोढुम्
अदृष्टपूर्वं हृषितः अस्मि दृष्ट्वा भयेन च प्रव्यथितं मनः मे
तत् एव मे दर्शय देव रूपं प्रसीद देवेश जगत् निवास

'Krishna, you are that special *Purush*, oldest of the old, only source of this world, you are the knower and that which needs to be known, by you this whole universe is permeated. You were there before *Vayu, Yam, Agni, Varun, Chandra, Prajapati and Brahma-* you are, indeed, the grandfather of them all. I did not understand all this, earlier, and I treated you like a friend and, maybe, I may have made some friendly and unflattering remarks about you. Please fogive me for all that'. He goes on, 'There is no one who equals you in all the three worlds, there is no question of anyone excelling you. Therefore, I am bowing to your feet, please bless me. The way a father forgives his children, the way a friend forgives a friend and the way a lover forgives the beloved, in the same way, please forgive me for all my acts of commission and omission'. A complete pall of *Bhakti* has taken over Arjun. त्वया ततं विश्वं , all of this universe is permeated by you, has been expressed similarly in Chhandogya Upanishad as सर्वं खलु इदम् ब्रह्म (३:१४:१), *That Brahman is all this.* 'you are, indeed, the grandfather of them all' has similarly been expressed in Shwetashwatar Upanishad (श्वेताश्वतर उपनिषद) as follows (६:७):

तं ईश्वरणाम् परमं महेश्वरम् तं देवतानाम् परमं च दैवतम्
पतिम् पतीनाम् परमं परस्ताद् विदाम देव भुवनेशम् ईड्यम

Krishna understands that Arjun has begun to repose his complete trust in the abilities of his leadership. He, now, tries to fortify the gains he has made, so far, by saying, 'न अहम् वेदैः न तपसा न दानेन न च इज्यया', people cannot realize me only by studying Vedas or by *Tapasya*, uninterrupted contemplation or by giving charity or by performing *Yagya*. O, Arjun, only through *Ananya Bhakti*, a devotion unlike any other, I can be realized and known- 'भक्त्या तु अनन्या शक्यः अहम् एवंविधः अर्जुन'(११:५ ४).

Now, Arjun has seen the temporally bound form of Krishna as his peer and spiritual mentor. He has also experienced, now, the time transcendent *Brahman*, which is beyond form. How was he able to experience the time transcendent *Brahman* can be a matter of conjecture. However, it is possible for a person, through the process of *Yoga*, to go beyond time and space and feel one and connected with the cosmos. Modern day scientitists are doing research in the functioning of the human brain in a *Yogic* meditational transcendence. Some day, we will have a clearer answer to Arjun's experience.

However, Arjun must be, now, filled with another question: should he focus on the temporal form of Krishna or the time transcendent reality? This is exactly the topic of the following conversation.

Chapter-XII
The Twelfth Question of Arjun

अर्जुनस्य द्वादशः प्रश्नः

Krishna had responded to Arjun's last question by concluding, 'I can be realized and known through *Ananya Bhakti* - भक्त्या तु अनन्या शक्यः अहम् एवंविधः अर्जुन (११:५ ८)'. Arjun is again confused: who should he focus upon? Should he focus his *Bhakti* on temporally bound Krishna, who has a physical form in this world? Or should he focus on *Brahman*, who is Time-Transcendent, unexpressed and unmanifest (अव्यक्तम्) in this world and, therefore, indestructible (अक्षरम्)? Should he try to realize his spiritual goal through devotion to a *time-trapped* form or to a *time-unbounded* abstraction? In this state of confusion, Arjun asks his twelfth question, 'who have a superior in knowledge of *Yoga* (तेषां के योगवित्तमाः) - those who are devoted to you or those who are devoted to *Brahman*?'

एवं सततयुक्ताः ये भक्ताः त्वां परिउपासते
ये च अपि अक्षरम् अव्यक्तम् तेषां के योगवित्तमाः (१२:१)

Despite the fact that Krishna had granted Arjun *Divya Drishti* so that he could experience Krishna's true, Time-Transcendent form, Arjun still appears to make a distinction between Krishna and *Brahman*. Krishna responds:

मयि आवेश्य मनः ये मां नित्ययुक्ताः उपासते
श्रद्धया परया उपेताः ते मे युक्ततमाः मताः (१२:२)

'In my view', Krishna says, 'those who meditate upon my temporal *Shyamsundar* form regularly with *Nirguna* devotion (परया श्रद्धया उपेताः) certainly have a great knowledge of *Yoga*'. *Nirguna* devotion is one of the four types of devotion (श्रद्धा) as outlined in Shrimad-Bhagawat (श्रीमद्भागवत):

सात्विकी आध्यात्मिकी श्रद्धा कर्मश्रद्धा तु राजसी
तामस्य धर्मे या श्रद्धा मत् सेवायां तु निर्गुणा (११:२५ :२७)

Devotion to, *Shraddha* (श्रद्धा) in, understanding the nature of *Atman* is called *Satvik Shraddha*. That which is engaged in performing worldly duties, *Karma-Kand* (कर्मकांड), is called *Rajasik*; that which is engaged in performing unlawful acts, *Adharma* (अधर्म), is called *Tamasik*. The fourth type of devotion which is engaged in understanding 'me' is called *Nirguna* (निर्गुण) devotion. As has been described, earlier, in the *Purush-Prakriti* model, Figure 8.1, Prakriti has all the three attributes- Satvik, Rajasik and Tamasik but Purush is beyond all the three attributes. It is attribute-less (निर्गुण), i.e., *it is beyond id, ego and super ego*. Therefore, it is recommended that those who want to understand the 'special' *Purush*, and, ultimately, the *Brahman*, must go beyond the *Prakriti Tatva* and its three attributes. This is a 'must do' step in realizing *Brahman*. Krishna, however, also adds this:

ये तु अक्षरम् निर्देश्यम् अव्यक्तम् परि उपासते
सर्वत्रगम् अचिन्त्यम् च कूटस्थम् अचलम् ध्रुवम् (१२:३)

संनियम्य इन्द्रियग्रामं सर्वत्र समबुद्धयः
ते प्राप्नुवन्ति मामं एव सर्वभूत हिते रताः (१२:४)

Those who, after controlling their sense organs, become unprejudiced (समबुद्धयः) to things which are different; those who are engaged in the welfare of all beings (सर्वभूत हिते रताः); those who are devoted to that which goes everywhere (सर्वत्रग), the unmanifest (अव्यक्त), that which is beyond all thought, that which is Time-Transcendent (कूटस्थ), immovable

(अचल), and indestructible (अक्षर), all of them also understand me. Krishna is not claiming that he is *Brahman*, what he is saying is that those who have travelled as far as realizing the *Purush Tatva* of Figure 8.1, they are actually only a short distance away from realizing *Brahman*. In a way, the path to the realization of *Brahman* passes through the milestone of realization of *Purush*. Arriving there has other previous milestones like controlling sense organs, rising above 'seeing things differently with prejudice' and rising above the three attributes- *Satvik, Rajasik and Tamasik*- all of which imply going beyond the *Prakriti Tatva*. It is also noteworthy that contradictory qualities have been ascribed to *Brahman*. That 'goes everywhere' (सर्वत्रग), but That is also immovable (अचल). Similar contradictory aspects of Brahman have also been expressed in Ishavasya-Upanishad (ईशावास्य उपनिषद) as follows (८ :५):

अनेजत् एकम् मनसः जवीयः न एनत् देवाः आप्नुवन् पूर्वम् अर्षत्
तत् धावतः अन्यान् अत्येति तिष्ठत् तस्मिन् अपः मातरिश्वा दधाति
तत् एजति तत् न एजति तत् दूरे तत् उ अन्तिके
तत् अन्तरस्य सर्वस्य तत् उ सर्वस्य अस्य बाह्यतः

That does not move, yet That is faster than the mind; That cannot be grasped by physical sense organs (देवाः) because That is beyond all of them; That can overtake other moving objects even if That is immovable. That walks, yet That does not walk; That is far, yet That is near; That is inside everything, yet That is outside everything. As a side note, that which illuminates is called *Deva* (देव), द्योतयन्ति इति देवाः, however, here the word *Deva* (देव) means sense organs because sense organs 'illuminate' their subjects (विषय). It is also noteworthy that the Persian word *khoda* is derived from the same Sanskrit root- *kham dyotayati iti khoda* (खम् द्योतयति इति खोदा), that which illuminates the sky is *khoda*.

So what does an ordinary person make out of these riddle-like, contradictory aspects of *Brahman*? These aspects of have been called *Saguna* (सगुण) and *Nirguna* (निर्गुण) aspects or *Sopadhik* (सोपधिक) and *Nirupadhik* (निरुपाधिक) aspects. That aspect which is beyond the three attributes (त्रिगुण)) is called *Nirguna* (निर्गुण) and that which has not gone beyond them is called *Sagun* (सगुण). Krishna's *Shyamsundar* form, for example, is a good representation of *Brahman's Saguna* aspects, whereas 'that which goes everywhere (सर्वत्रग), that which is the unmanifest (अव्यक्त), that which is beyond all thought, that which is Time-Transcendent (कूटस्थ), immovable (अचल) and indestructible (अक्षर)', is a good description of *Nirguna* aspects. Krishna has established equivalency between the meditation on *Saguna* aspects and *Nirguna* aspects and meditating on either of these two will be helpful in the path of realization of *Atman* and *Brahman*. The question, 'who have a superior knowledge of *Yoga* (तेषां के योगवित्तमाः) - those who are devoted to you(the *Saguna* form) or those who are devoted to *Brahman* (the *Nirguna* form)', has been responded to at this stage. The answer is: neither of them is superior to the other. They are two equivalent paths both leading to the realization of *Atman* and *Brahman*.

However, Krishna realizes that it is very difficult for an ordinary person like Arjun to visualize the *Nirguna*, attributeless, aspects. Theferfore, he advises Arjun thus:

ये तु सर्वाणि कर्माणि मयि संन्यस्य मत्परः
अनन्येन एव योगेन मां ध्यायन्त उपासते (१२:६)
तेषां अहम् समुद्धर्ता मृत्यु संसार सागरात्
भवामि न चिरात् पार्थ मयि आवेशित चेतसाम् (१२:७)

अथ च,
मयि एव मन आधत्स्व मयि मयि बुद्धिं निवेशय
निवसिष्यसि मयि एव अत उद्‌र्ध्वम् न संशयः (१२:८)

'Those who relegate all *Karma* to Krishna (which is close to engaging in Nishkam Karma) and meditate with *Ananya* (अनन्या) devotion on him, they surely go beyond the *Prakritik* cycle of birth and death and, thus, they realize *Atman*. Arjun, focus on my *Shyamsundar* (श्यामसुन्दर) form and dedicate your thinking to me. By doing this, you will surely 'co-habit' with me- there is no doubt about it'. Krishna understands that it would be easier for Arjun to visualize the *Saguna* form, that is why he is recommending this path to Arjun.

Another key point which is inherent in Krishna's response to the twelfth question is the importance of not being prejudiced (समबुद्धयः) to things just because they are different. Mind needs to be trained to see beyond the difference in different looking, different feeling things. As long as a person is still at the level of perceiving difference and not the underlying unity in this world, that person will find it difficult to achieve the goal of realizing *Atman*. This viewpoint also finds a great prominence in Ishavasya-Upanishad (ईशावास्य उपनिषद) as follows (६:७):

यः तु सर्वाणि भूतानि आत्मनि एव अनुपश्यति
सर्वभूतेषु च आत्मानं ततः न विजुगुप्सते (६)
यस्मिन् सर्वाणि भूतानि आत्मा एव अभूत् विजानतः
तत्र कः मोहः कः शोकः एकत्वम् अनुपश्यतः (७)

The person who 'sees' all beings in *Atman* and *Atman* in all beings, that person does not hate anyone or anything (न विजुगुप्सते). Furthermore, when a person reaches such a stage where all beings look like *Atman* and vice versa, then, attachment (Moh, मोह) and grief (Shok, शोक) do not mean much for such a person.

In his response to the most recent question, Kirshna has tried to establish two things: one, it does not matter whether a person focuses on the temporal form or on the time transcendent reality, they both lead to *Nirvana*. Secondly, it also very important for a person to elevate one's consciousness beyond perceptible differences in this world. Krishna also implies that a person can gradually move from meditating on *saguna* to *nirguna* and to, subsequently, realizing *Brahman*. It is not a question of either or. Both paths lead to the same spiritual goal.

Chapter-XIII
The Thirteenth Question of Arjun

अर्जुनस्य त्रयोदशः प्रश्नः

Let's pause for a moment and take a stock of where Arjun is in his quest to realize the nature of *Atman* and *Brahman*. To begin with, Arjun was sufficiently disinclined to fight in the war due to his concern for killing his own kith and kin. He did not want a victory which was an outcome of a horrific war where people, who were very close to him, were going to be hurt and killed. Krishna's challenge was how to get him to fight in the war. To achieve his goals, Krishna introduced a concept of something which is beyond death and destruction. He talked about something which is beyond Time and its measuremeant and which is, thus, Time-Transcendent (अकाल). That something is everywhere; that something is in everything and that something can be understood and realized through a process of *Yoga*, a process which helps one to realize the nature of *Atman* and *Brahman*.

Krishna, then, talked about the five sense organs- ears, skin, eyes, tongue and nose- and their five subjects, the *tanmatras* (तन्मात्रा) - शब्द, स्पर्श, रुप, रस, गन्ध - sound, touch, form, taste and smell. He emphasized, again and again, the importance of the human consciousness rising above the subjects of the five senses. He considered the attainment of such a state of mind a major milestone in the process of spiritual quest. Then he advised Arjun to work steadfastly towards rising above one's ascription of doer-ship of deeds (अस्मिता) and, then, above Prakriti's *Satvik, Rajasik and Tamasik* attributes.

Along the way, he had also pointed out difficulties, largely due to the natural tendencies, *Vrittis* (वृत्ति), of the human mind and the powerful attraction between the sense organs and *tanmatras*, their subjects, in attaining major milestones. He also introduced the concepts of *Nishkam Karma* and *Bhakti* as potential tools to disconnect sense organs from their *tanmatras*. That's where Arjun is right now. He appears to be mentally prepared, now, to achieve the next major milestone from an intellectual and spiritual point of view.

One would wonder that Arjun already had a heavy dose of spiritual concepts. However, he does not seem to feel so as he asks, 'Krishna, I want to know more about all of these: *Prakriti* (प्रकृति), *Purush* (पुरुष), *Kshetra* (क्षेत्र), *Kshetragya* (क्षेत्रज्ञ), knowledge (ज्ञान) and 'that which must be known and understood' (ज्ञेय):

प्रकृतिं पुरुषम् च एव क्षेत्रं क्षेत्रज्ञम् एव च
एतद् ज्ञातुं इच्छामि ज्ञानम् ज्ञेयम् च केशव (१३:१)

Krishna replies:

इदम् शरीरम् कौन्तेय क्षेत्रम् इति अभिधीयते
एतद् यः वेत्ति तम् प्राहुः क्षेत्रज्ञ इति तद् विदः (१३:२)

Krishna starts with defining *Kshetra* (क्षेत्र) and *Kshetragya* (क्षेत्रज्ञ). This body (शरीर) is the *Kshetra* (क्षेत्र) and those who understand this are called *Kshetragya* (क्षेत्रज्ञ). In other words, this body (शरीर) which is the 'playground' for the play of senses and enactment of their satiation by their subjects, the *tanmatras*, is the *Khsetra* (क्षेत्र). Those who, in a *Karma-bounded* state, identify this body with their *Asmita*, the 'doer-ship' of doing, and those who, in a *Karma-unbounded* state and having risen above their *Asmita*, still, identify themselves with this body, both of them, are called *Kshetragya* (क्षेत्रज्ञ). Thus *Karma-bounded* (बद्धजीव) and *Karma-unbounded* (मुक्तजीव), both, whether they have risen above *Asmita or not*, are called *Kshetragya* (क्षेत्रज्ञ). They understand that this body can be a means for both- to attain *Moksha* (मोक्ष) and, thus, become unbounded by *Karma* or to remain as someone pursuing *Bhoga* (भोग) in a deeply *Karma-bounded* state. A key point to note is that those who mistakenly identify *Atman* with this body (शरीर) and pursue a path of attainment of wordly pleasures, *Bhoga* (भोग), are certianly not *Kshetragya* (क्षेत्रज्ञ). This in itself is not bad, however, for such persons, though, it would be extremely difficult for them to realize the true nature of *Atman* and *Brahman*. It is important to keep the observer independent of the object being observed. In Shrimad-Bhagawat (श्रीमद्भागवत) this independence of the observer and the object being observed has been described thus:

अदन्ति च एकम् फलम् अस्य गृध्रा ग्रामेचरः एकम् अरण्यवाराः
हंसा यः एकं बहुरूपम् इज्यैः मायामयम् वेद सः वेद वेदम् (११:१२:२३)

'One is eating the fruits with great enjoyment, while the other is indifferent to all this', this is the way Shrimad-Bhagawat puts it. Smriti (स्मृति) describes the same thing differently,

क्षेत्राणि हि शरीरगणि बीजं च अपि शुभ अशुभे
तानि वेत्ति सः योग आत्मा ततः क्षेत्रज्ञ उच्यते

All this physical manifestation, the body (शरीर), is, truly, the *Kshetra* (क्षेत्र) and the *Karma*, which is based either on *Dharma* (धर्म) or on *Adharma* (अधर्म), is like a causative seed (बीज) of this physical maninfestation. Those who understand this are called *Kshetragya* (क्षेत्रज्ञ). Figure 13.1 ties all these key concepts together. As shown in the figure, 'memory of the enjoyment' (आशय) of the fruits of *Karma* (कर्म), is a potent binding force (बन्धन), which is of three types- *Prakritik* (प्राकृतिक), *Vaikarik* (वैकारिक) and *Dakshina* (दक्षिणा). A person becomes and remains *Karma-bounded* (कर्मबद्ध) as a result of not only the *Karma* itself but also as a result of memory of the enjoyment of the fruits of the *Karma*. Such a person is called a *Baddha-Jiva* (बद्धजीव), a *banda*, and the person who has risen above this is called *Mukta-Jiva* (मुक्तजीव), *kha-banda*. Both, the *Baddha-Jiva* (बद्धजीव) and the *Mukta-Jiva* (मुक्तजीव), are called *Kshetragya* (क्षेत्रज्ञ), because both of them have the capability, if they choose to exercise that capability, to understand the true nature of *Atman* and *Brahman*. A *Baddha-Jiva* (बद्धजीव), though, goes through the cycle of birth, life and the living (जन्म, आयु, भोग) in this world (संसार), several times, until the capability to get rid of the potent 'binding force', the *Bandhan* (बन्धन), is successfully exercised. Then the *banda* becomes *kha-banda*; *Baddha* becomes *Mukta*. *Nirvana* is achieved.

Krishna further tells Arjun more about *Kshetra* and *Kshetragya*, 'hear some more, in summary, though, about what is that *Kshetra*; how does it look like; what are its evolutes; with what objective has it manifested and what has it been manifested from. I will, also, tell you more about *Kshetragya* and its form and its power', तत् क्षेत्रम् यत् च यादृक् च यत् विकारि यतः च यत्, सः च यः यत् प्रभावः च तत् समासेन में श्रृणु (१३:८). This is where Krishna introduces a model of life which progressively moves from a physical layer to a spiritual layer and which has been first illustrated, earlier, in the *Purush-Prakriti* model. He tells Arjun about twenty five *tatvas* (Purush, Prakriti, Mahat, Asmita, the mind, five sense organs- eyes, ears,

The Spirit of One

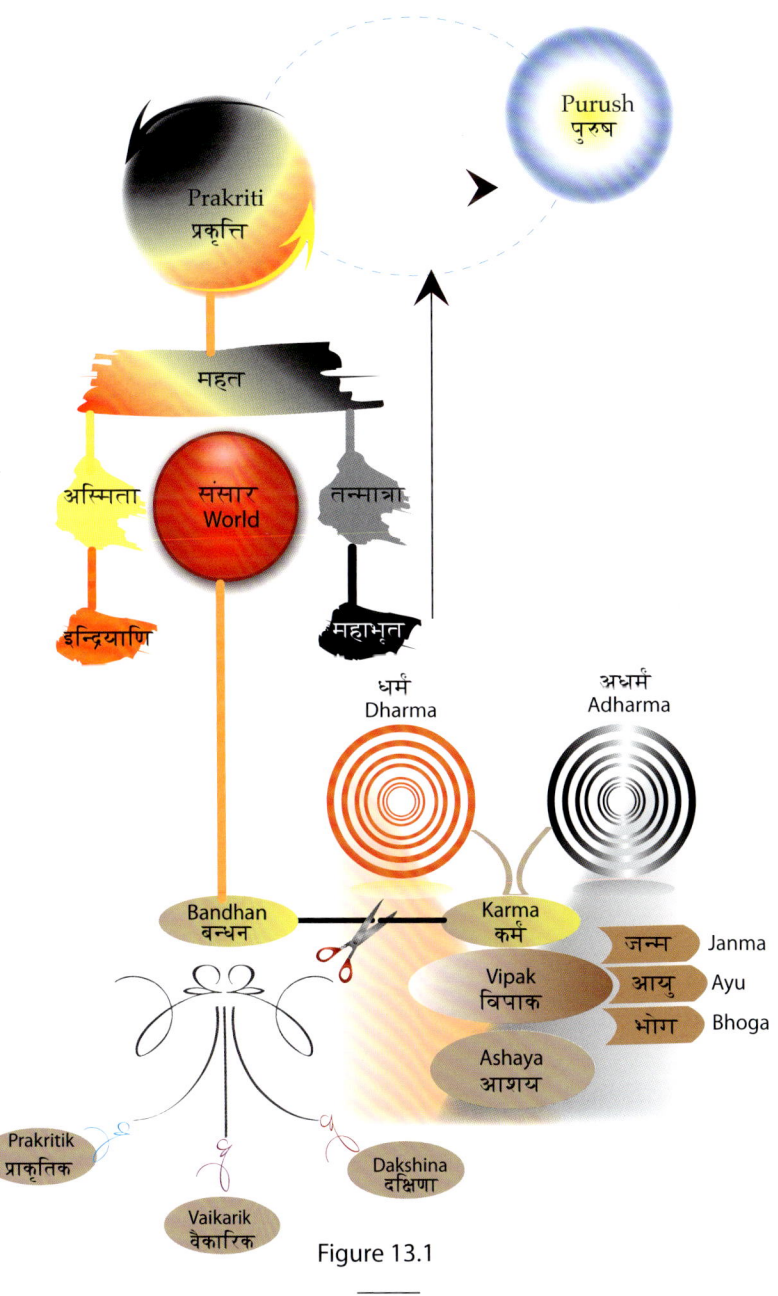

Figure 13.1

nose, tounge and skin; five motor organs- hands, feet, speech, anus, genitives; five *tanmatras*-form, taste, smell, touch, sound; and five *mahabhuts*-earth, water, fire, air, sky). All *tatvas*, except the *Purush tatva*, are collectively called *Kshetra* (क्षत्र). Those who understand this are called *Kshetragya* (क्षत्रज्ञ).

Another part of Arjun's question revolves around the topic of knowledge (ज्ञान) and 'that which must be known and understood(ज्ञेय)'. He says, 'ज्ञातुं इच्छामि ज्ञानम् ज्ञेयम् च केशव (१३:१)', I want to know what is knowledge and what is to be known. Krishna has a long list of twenty items which, according to him, are examples of knowledge (ज्ञान)- absence of uncalled for pride (मानशून्यता), absence of obstinacy (दम्भहीनता), non-violence (अहिंसा), forgiveness (क्षान्ति), simplicity (सरलता), respect for the teacher (आचार्य उपासन), internal and external purity (शौच), steadfastness of mind (स्थैर्य), control of one's sense organs (आत्म विनिग्रह), detachment from the subjects of sense organs (इन्द्रिय अर्थ वैराग्य), absence of arrogance (अहंकार शून्यता), critical reflection on birth-death-old age-disease-sorrow (जन्म,मृत्यु,जरा,व्याधि, दुःख अनुदर्शन), detachment from children-spouse-material possessions (पुत्र,दार,गृह असक्ति), neutral state of mind in sorrow and happiness (अनभिष्वङ्ग), equibalance of mind during prosperity and adversity (इष्ट अनिष्ट समचित्तत्व), a complete devotion towards me (अनन्या भक्ति), a liking for seclusion (निर्जनवास), disinterest in the company of sense driven people (जनसंसदि अरुचि), a continuous, critical reflection on the subject of *Atman* (अध्यात्मज्ञान नित्यत्वम्), a critical reflection on how to attain *Moksha* (तत्वज्ञान अर्थदर्शनम्). That which should be known and understood is as follows:

ज्ञेयं यत् तत् प्रवक्ष्यामि यत् ज्ञात्वा अमृतम् अश्नुते
अनादि मत् परं ब्रह्म न सत् तत् न असत् उच्यते (१३:१३)

'And that *Brahman* (ब्रह्म), by knowing which, *Moksha* (अमृतमं), time transcendence, is attained, is without beginning (अनादि), beyond existence (न सत्) and beyond non-existence (न असत्)'.

Every evolute has an evolent; everything which exists now was something which it is not now. Krishna is saying that *Brahman* is that thing which is neither an evolute nor an evolent; it is neither an event nor a cause of an event. Brahman is beyond time-space event horizon. Upon understanding this, it is possible for a person's knowledge of the empirical world to go beyond the knowledge of birth, life and living (जन्म, आयु, भोग). This is the true knowledge (ज्ञान) and *Brahman* is the true 'knowable' (ज्ञेय). Furthermore, although there is a partial qualitative similarity between *Atman* and *Brahman* and that's why, sometimes, *Jiva* (जीव) has been referred to as *Brahm-Bhut* (ब्रह्म-भूत) or *Brahm-Bhuyay* (ब्रह्म-भूयाय), it is worthy to note that *Jiva's* consciousness is a sort of molecular, biological, consciousness (अणु चैतन्य), whereas, *Brahman* is self-illumined, self conscious (पूर्ण चेतन). Because *Brahman* is beyond existence and beyond non-existence and, therefore, its consciousness is not biological. Brahman is beyond *Karma-bounded Jiva-Atman* and *Karma-unbounded Param-Atman*.

Chhandogya-Upanishad (छान्दोग्य उपनिषद) describes the same *Brahman* as follows, 'सर्वम् खलु इदम् ब्रह्म ... सर्वकर्मा, सर्वकामः, सर्वगन्धः, सर्वरसः, सर्वम् इदम्.... (३:१८:१-३)', all of this, which is all-pervasive, is *Brahman*. Krishna throws some more light on that which should be known and understood as follows:

सर्व इन्द्रिय गुण आभासम् सर्व इन्द्रिय विवर्जितम्
असक्तम् सर्व भृत् च एव निर्गुणं गुणभोक्तृ च (१३:१५)

That is the illuminator of all the sense organs and their subjects, however, that is itself without all *Prakrit* (प्राकृत) sense organs ; that is itself without attachment, however, that serves everyone; that is 'beyond the three *gunas*' (निर्गुण), however, that enjoys all the six *Aishwarya* (ऐश्वर्य) gunas known as *Bhag* (भग) and that is why that is called *Bhagavan* (भगवान).

Ken-Upanishad (केन उपनिषद) also affirms this, तत् चक्षुषः चक्षुः (१:२)', That is the eye of all the eyes'. And, Shwetashwatar Upanishad (श्वेताश्वतर उपनिषद) also declares thus, 'अपाणिपादो जवनो गृहिता पश्यति अचक्षुः सः श्रृणोति अकर्णः (३:१९)', *Brahman* does not have *Prakrit* (प्राकृत) hand and feet, still that can hold things and that is mobile; that sees without eyes and that hears without ears. And some more, 'बहिः अन्तः च भूतानाम् अचरम् चरम् एव च, सूक्ष्मत्वात् तत् अविज्ञेयम् दूरस्थं च अन्तिके च तत्(१३:१६)', that is inside as well as outside everything; that is hard to experience because that is the subtlest among the subtle; that is, at the same time, near and afar.

Mundak Upanishad (मुण्डक उपनिषद) declares thus, 'दूरात् सुदूरे तदिहान्तिके च पश्यत् स्विहैव निहितम् गुहायाम् (३:१:७)', that is farther than the farthest and nearer than the nearest. But those who are capable of 'seeing' can experience that *Brahman* in their own heart. Krishna emphasizes an element of unity of the whole universe by saying this,

अविभक्तम् च भूतेषु विभक्तम् इव च स्थितम्
भूत भर्तृ च तत् ज्ञेयम् ग्रसिष्णु प्रभविष्णु च (१३:१७)

That is indivisible, yet that is divided into all beings by the virtue of being in all beings. By the virtue of this divisibility in indivisibility, the universe comes together (प्र भविष्णु), stays together (भूतभर्तृ) and, then, becomes indivisible

एक एव पर: विष्णु: सर्वत्र अपि न संशय

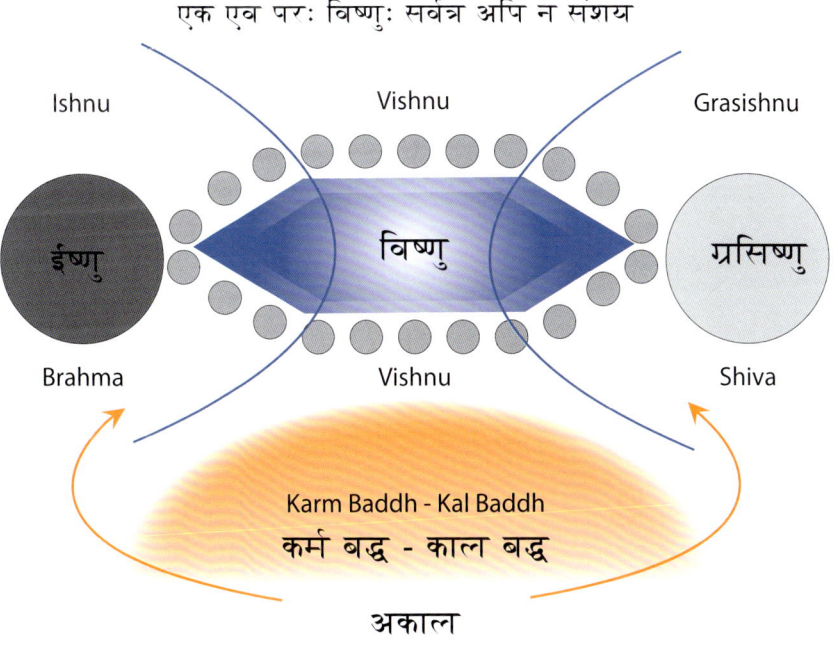

Time Transcendent
Figure 13.2

again (ग्रसिष्णु). These are the *Brahma*, *Vishnu* and *Mahesh (Shiva)* aspects of one *Brahman*- 'एक एव पर: विष्णु: सर्वत्र अपि न संशय:', same and only one Vishnu is everywhere, there is no doubt about it, thus declare the Smritis (स्मृति). Figure 13.2 depicts this in a clearer way, where the three aspects of the same Time-Transcedent reality have been shown. Time-Transcedence is *Brahma*(Ishnu, Akal) before temporal manifestation of a being; it is *Vishnu*(Ram, Krishna) during the temporal manifestation and it is *Mahesh* (Shiva, Grasishnu, Maha-Kal) after dissolution into Time-Transcendence again. Krishna affirms his response by saying, 'इति क्षेत्रम् तथा ज्ञानम्

ज्ञेयम् च उक्तम् समासतः (१३:१°)', that is how *Kshetra* (क्षेत्रम्), knowledge (ज्ञानम्) and that which should be known (ज्ञेयम्) can be summarily (समासतः) described.

Now, having talked about *Kshetra* (क्षेत्रम्), knowledge (ज्ञानम्) and that which should be known (ज्ञेयम्), Krishna is throwing more light on the nature of *Prakriti* and *Purush* of Figure 13.1, thus:

प्रकृतिं पुरुषम् च एव विद्धि अनादि उभौ अपि
विकारान् च गुणान् च एव विद्धि प्रकृति सम्भवान् (१३:२०)

He says, 'both- *Prakriti* and *Purush*- are without beginning, i.e., they did not have a past and they will not have a future and, for them, time, 't=0', is extended in both temporal directions and, therefore, they are everpresent. Everything which has temporal dimensions came of them and they are, all, evolutes of *Prakriti- Prakriti's Vikriti*, complete with the three attributes- *Satvik, Rajasik and Tamasik*.'

Elsewhere, too, he has referred to this model, 'भूमिः आपः अनलः वायुः खम् मनः बुद्धिः एव च, अहङ्कार इति इयम् मे भिन्ना प्रकृति अष्टधा (७:८) and 'अपरा इयम् इतः तु अन्यां प्रकृतिं विद्धि मे परम्, जीवभूताम् महाबाहो यया इदम् धार्यते जगत्(७:५)', The five *Mahabhut*- Earth (भूमिः), Water (आपः), Fire (अनलः), Air (वायुः), and Sky (खम्)-, Ahankar (Mahat and Asmita together, अहङ्कार) Mind(मनः) and Wisdom (बुद्धिः)- these are eight *Apara* (अपरा) components of *Prakriti* and I, the *Purush tatva*, the *Para-Shakti* (परा शक्ति), I am beyond all this, by which this universe is sustained (विष्णु), यया इदम् धार्यते जगत्(७:५)'. Here mind (मनः) and wisdom (बुद्धिः) have been counted separately, however, in the context of Figure 13.1, they should be understood one and the same. Furthermore, Krishna states:

एतत् योनीनि भूतानि सर्वाणि इति उपधारय
अहम् कृत्स्नस्य जगतः प्रभवः प्रलयः तथा (७:६)

'Undesrtand, Arjun, all this empirical and temporal world has come out of the union of these two- *Prakriti* and *Purush*. I am the source of emanation (प्रभवः,ईष्णु) and the sink for dissolution (प्रलयः, ग्रसिष्णु) of all this'.

Out of these two- *Prakriti and Purush- Prakriti* is said to be the source of the evolent-evolute duo and *Purush*, when in the form of a *Baddha-Jiva* (बद्धजीव), is said to be the context for happiness-sorrow duo, 'कार्य कारण कर्तृत्वे हेतुः प्रकृतिः उच्यते, पुरुषः सुखदुःखानां भोक्तृत्वे हेतुः उच्यते (१३:२१)'. As has been previously discussed, in the context of the eighth question, the 'eternal in itself' and the 'eternal in the empirical flux' are the *Adhiyagya* and *Adhideva* respectively. *Adhiyagya* manifestation, in a *Karma-bound* (कर्म बद्ध) and *Time-bound* (काल बद्ध) state, is called *Adhibhut*. While *Adhibhut* is the context for the happiness-sorrow duo, the *Adhiyagya* is a disspassionate onlooker in all beings which are all united, by the same principle, in their diversity, 'यदा भूत पृथक् भावम् एकस्थम् अनुपश्यति, तत एव च विस्तारं ब्रह्म संपद्यते तदा (१३:३१)', when a person understands that the attributes of all beings, though different looking, are also in the same *Prakriti* and have come from the same *Prakriti*, then, that perosn is close to understanding the true nature of *Brahman*. And that *Param Atman*, in the form of *Adhiyagya*, the disspassionate onlooker, even by being inside a being, is neither the 'doer' of anything nor the 'enjoyer' of the outcome of the deeds done , 'शरीरस्थः अपि कौन्तेय न करोति न लिप्यते (१३:३२)'.

As one can see the ground for getting Arjun out of his dilemna appears to have been sufficiently prepared. Krishna has walked him through a spiritual model of human existence to a point where Arjun can take the next big leap and engage in the lawful and just war. Even if Arjun kills his kith and kin, the central point of his dilemna, in the war, it will be the *Adhibhut* who will be actually doing the killing and *Adhiyagya*, the dispassionate onlooker, will be unaffected by all this. Since *Adhiyagya*, the manifestation of the *Adhideva*, the eternal in the empirical flux, is the eternal in itself, there should be no ground for Arjun to ascribe to his 'real' self the doership of the aweful act of destruction in the war. This connection between the *Adhiyagya* and *Adhideva* also constitutes a strong basis for *Nishkam Karma*.

Chaptcr-XIV
The Fourteenth Question of Arjun

अर्जुनस्य चतुर्दशः प्रश्नः

कैः लिङ्गैः त्रीन् गुणान् एतान् अतीतः भवति प्रभो
किम् आचारः कथं च एतान् त्रीन् गुणान् अतिवर्त्तते (१४:२१)

Krishna has asserted that *Prakriti* is a sort of a great womb and that it is he who, dispassionately (तटस्थ), sows the *Prabhav* (प्रभवः,ईषणु) seeds, for all beings, in that womb and, thus, all beings are born in a time-bound and *karma-bound* form. 'तस्मिन् गर्भम् ददामि अहम् (१४:३)', I help *Prakriti* to 'conceive'. In response to how does a person become *karma-bound* and, therefore, one cannot 'un-attach' oneself from the evolutes of one's actions, Krishna says,

Prakriti's three attributes (त्रिगुण)- *Satva* (सत्वम्), *Raj* (रजः) *and Tam* (तमः) - are the ones which 'tie' the imperishable (अव्ययम्) *Adhiyagya*, the eternal in itself, in this body (देह) to the evolutes of its *Karma*, as shown in Figure 14.1. Same three *Prakritik* attributes have earlier been noted as *Satvik, Rajasik and Tamasik*. Shwetashwatar Upanishad (श्वेताश्वतर उपनिषद, ४:५) conveys the same thought as follows:

अजाम् एकां लोहित शुक्ल कृष्णां बह्वीः प्रजाः सृजमानां सरूपाः
अजः हि एकः जुषमाणः अनुशेते जहाति एनां भुक्तभोगां अजः अन्यः

Purush and *Prakriti* are, both, unborn (अज). However, one unborn (अज), the *Purush*, 'unites' with the other unborn (अजा), the *Prakriti*, which has three *Gunas* (त्रिगुण)- *Satvik, Rajasik and Tamasik*, portrayed as red, white and black colours, respectively, in the above verse. *Satvik* (सत्वम्) attribute

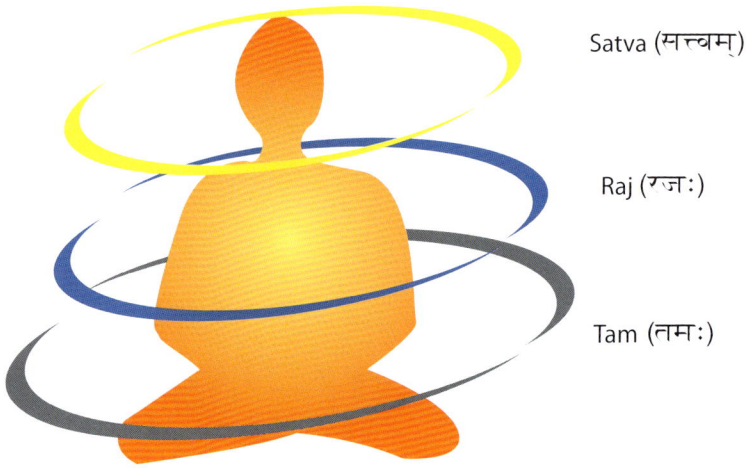

Figure 14.1

of *Prakriti* binds a being through the bond of happiness and knowledge, ie, the attachment to the sense of well-being and being knowledgeable embodied in statements like 'I am happy', 'I have knowledge'. *Rajasik* (रज:) attribute is born of excessive attachment and it binds a being through desire for and attachment to *Karma* and its evolutes- रजो रागात्मकम् विद्धि तृष्णा सङ्ग समुद्भवम् (१४:७). The third attribute, *Tamasik* (तम:), is born of ignorance and it binds a being through *Pramad* (प्रमाद), *Alasya* (आलस्य) and *Nidra* (निद्रा). Krishna further states,

गुणान् एतान् अतीत्य त्रीन् देही देहसमुद्भवान्
जन्म मृत्यु जरा दु:खै: विमुक्त: अमृतम् अश्नुते (१४:२०)

After going beyond these three *gunas* by overcoming them, a person becomes *Karma-unbound* and becomes free from birth, death, old age and sorrow (जन्म मृत्यु जरा दु:खै: विमुक्त:)

and attains *Moksha* (अमृतम् अश्नुते). It is worth recalling Figure 4.4, from Chapter-IV, the three types of *Bandhans* as shown in Figure 14.2:

What Krishna has described here embodies the three types of *Bandhans* of Figure 14.2- *Prakritik, Vaikarik and Dakshina* as explained, earlier, in Chapter-IV. It is also worth recalling that there are two major steps in spiritual realization- *Apar-Vairagya*, which is a state of desirelessness for worldly and non-worldly things, विषय वैतृष्ण्यम्, and *Par-Vairagya*, which is rising above the three *gunas*, गुणवैतृष्ण्यम्. Patanjali's Yoga-Sutra defines these as follows: दृष्टानुश्रविक विषय वितृष्णस्य वशीकार संज्ञा वैराग्यम् (१:१५) and तत्परं पुरुषख्यातेः गुणवैतृष्ण्यम् (१:१६). Upon hearing such an assertive declaration and such a great praise

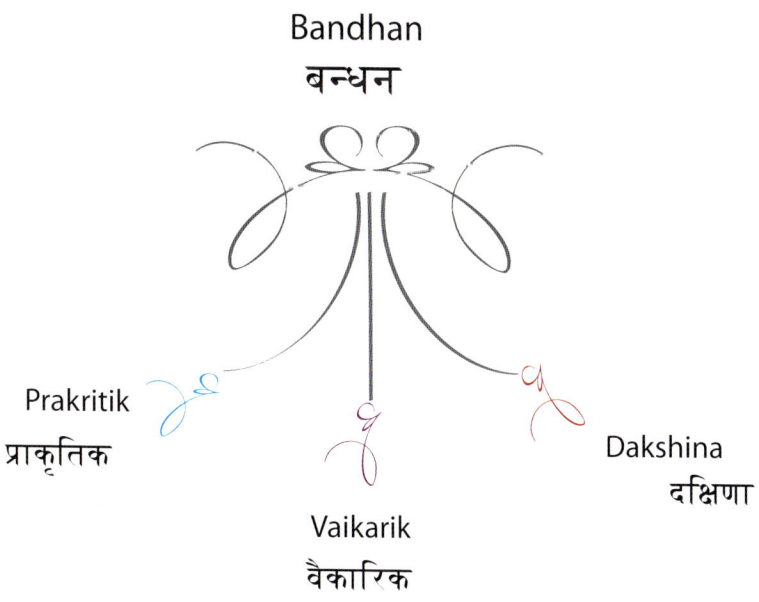

Bandhan
बन्धन

Prakritik
प्राकृतिक

Dakshina
दक्षिणा

Vaikarik
वैकारिक

Figure 14.2

for the virtue of rising above the three *gunas* and becoming a *Guna-Vitrishna* (गुण वितृष्ण), Arjun asks the fourteenth question, 'Krishna, tell me, what are the qualities of such a person who has risen above these three *gunas*; how does that person behave and how does that person attain such a state?' Krishna is ready with an answer,

प्रकाशम च प्रवृत्तिम च मोहम एव च पाण्डव
न द्वेष्टि संप्रवृत्तानि न निवृत्तानि कांक्षति (१८:२२)

उदासीनवत् आसीनः गुणैः यः न विचाल्यते
गुणाः वर्तन्त इति एवम् यः अवतिष्ठति न इङ्गते (१८:२३)

समदुःखसुखः स्वस्थः सम लोष्ट अश्म काञ्चनः
तुल्य प्रिय अप्रियः धीरः तुल्य निन्दा आत्म संस्तुतिः (१८:२४)

मान अपमानयोः तुल्यः तुल्यः मित्र अरि पक्षयोः
सर्व आरम्भ परित्यागी गुण अतीतः सः उच्यत (१८:२५)

It is, indeed, a long feature list which can be summarized as follows: those who are unmoved by the evolutes of *gunas*- happiness and sorrow; those who are not prejudiced to different forms such as dirt, stone and gold; those who do not let praise or criticism by others get to their heads; those who treat friends and foes fairly and those who abdicate all *Karma* except those required for for living one's life, they are the ones who are called *guna-vitrishna* (गुण वितृष्ण) or *guna-atit* (गुण अतीत). After earning this qualification, a person is close to experiencing *Brahman*, सः गुणान् समतीत्य एतान् ब्रह्मभूयाय कल्पते (१८:२६). In Chhandogya Unpanishad (छान्दोग्य उपनिषद), eight features have been ascribed to such a *Brahm-bhut* (ब्रह्मभूत) person:

यः आत्मा अपहतपाप्मा विजरः विमृत्युः विशोकः विजिघित्सः
अपिपासः सत्यकामः सत्संकल्पः सः अन्वेष्टव्यः (८:७:१)

One who is without *Pap* (अपहतपाप्मा), without old age (विजर), without death (विमृत्यु), without grief (विशोक), without memory of satiation of desires (विजिघित्स), without desire (अपिपास), truth-seeking (सत्यकाम) and focused on the path of truth seeking (सत्संकल्प) is a *Brahm-bhut* (ब्रह्मभूत) person.

As shown in Figure 14.3, above, after achieving two major but difficult milestones, a person is fully prepared to realize *Brahman*. The process from start to finish is called *Yoga* (योग), a process which takes an *Adhibhut* on the journey to experience *Brahman*. It will not be overemphasizing the case

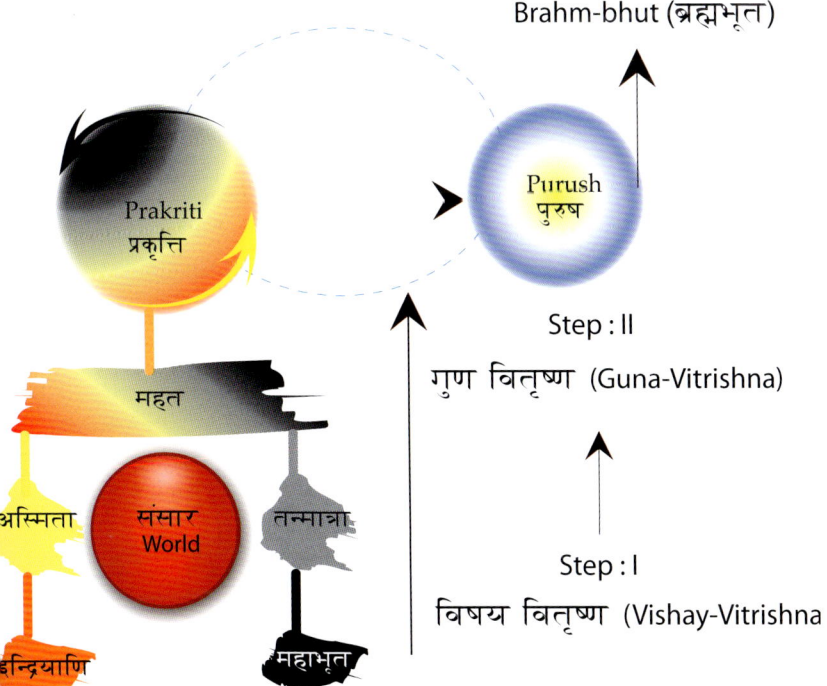

Figure 14.3

for attaining a state of गुण वितृष्ण (Guna-Vitrishna) before *Brahman* can be realized. Shrimad-Bhagawat (श्रीमद् भागवत) also states thus:

सान्त्विकः कारकः असङ्गी राग अन्धः राजसः स्मृतः
तामसः स्मृति विभृष्टः निर्गुणः मत् अपाश्रयः (११:२५:२६)

Those who are 'un-attached to *Karma*' (असङ्गी) and its evolutes are called *Satvik*; those who are 'blind in pursuing worldly pleasures' (राग अन्ध) are called *Rajasik* and those who do not know what is right and what is wrong, who display a sort of memory loss (स्मृति विभृष्ट), are called *Tamasik*. However, those who are above all these are called *Nirguna* (निर्गुण) and are qualified to realize *Brahman*. *Nirguna* (निर्गुण) or *Guna-Vitrishna* (गुण वितृष्ण) is a state where even attachment to knowledge and knowing ceases to exist. Just being unattached to the worldly (दृष्ट विषय) and non-worldly (अनुश्रविक विषय) subjects is not enough. Although that is an important and major milestone, as Patanjali has noted in Yoga-Sutra, 'दृष्टानुश्रविक विषय वितृष्णस्य वशीकार संज्ञा वैराग्यम् (१:१५). The complete process of Yoga has been described in Patanjali's Yoga-Sutra, in great detail, which can lead a person to go beyond the three *gunas*.

Chapter-XV
The Fifteenth Question of Arjun

अर्जुनस्य पञ्चदशः प्रश्नः

ये शास्त्रविधिम् उत्सृज्य यजन्ते श्रद्धया अन्विताः
तेषाम् निष्ठा तु का कृष्ण सत्त्वम् आहो रजः तमः (१७:१)

'O Krishna, what happens to those who do not follow the process of *Yoga* and who spend their time in prayers with great *Shraddha* (श्रद्धा)? Are they Satvik, Rajasik or Tamasik?' Basically, Arjun is after knowing a short-cut to rise above the three *Prakritik Gunas* and his question can be paraphrased as, 'for those who do not have time or intellectual qualification to go through the rigours of understanding Yogic methods, is there, perhaps, a simpler way to achieve the state of *Nirguna* (निर्गुण) or *Guna-Vitrishna* (गुण वितृष्ण)? For example, can those who spend time praying, with complete devotion, also attain the *Nirguna* state?

Krishna responds by saying that even *Shraddha* (श्रद्धा) is of three types- Satvik, Rajasik and Tamasik, 'त्रिविधा भवति श्रद्धा देहिनाम् सा स्वभावजा, सात्त्विकी राजसी च एव तामसी च इति ताम् श्रृणु (१७:२)'. These three types of *Shraddha* (श्रद्धा) are rooted in the kind of 'inside' (अन्तःकरण) tendency a person has and, also, what objectives a person has in mind, while offering one's prayers. Usually, Krishna continue, Satvik people worship *Deva* (देव), Rajasik people worship *Yaksha* (यक्ष) and *Rakshas* (राक्षस), while Tamasik people worship *Bhut-Pret* (भूत प्रेत), यजन्ते सात्त्विकाः देवान् यक्ष रक्षांसि राजसाः, प्रेतान् भूतगणान् च अन्ये यजन्ते तामसाः जनाः (१७:४)'. Some times, same *Deva* (देव) is worshipped in all three *gunas* with different objectives in mind. For example, at the time of dissolution of the universe, Markandey (मार्कण्डेय) worshipped Shiva so that he could preserve the knowledge of creation and he lived for one *Kalpa* (कल्प). This worship is called Satvik due to its profound goal of preserving the knowledge of creation. On the other hand, worship of Shiva by Ravan(रावण) and Vanasur (वाणासुर) is called Rajasik because it was done with an objective of acquiring power. Likewise, Bhashmasur's (भष्मासुर) worship of Shiva is called Tamasik due to his aweful objective. Krishna throws some more light on this as follows:

अफलाकांक्षिभिः यज्ञः विधिदिष्टः यः इज्यते
यष्टव्यम् एव इति मनः समाधाय सः सात्त्विकः (१७:११)

अभिसन्धाय तु फलम् दम्भार्थम् अपि च एव यत
इज्यते भरतश्रेष्ठ तम् यज्ञम् विद्धि राजसम् (१७:१२)

विधिहीनम् असृष्टान्नम् मन्त्रहीनम् अदक्षिणम्
श्रद्धा विरहितम् यज्ञम् तामसम् परिचक्षते (१७:१३)

The worship performed without being attached to the goal for the worship is called Satvik; that with attachment to the goal and with an intention to show off is called Rajasik worship. Tamasik worship is that which is performed without a proper process, without proper mantra and without devotion. Krishna, then, also talks about three kinds of *Tap* (तप) and *Dan* (दान) which also parallel the three types of worship. For example, he says, that the Dan (दान), charity, which is given to someone deserving (योग्य) and who is unable to return the favour in cash or kind is a *Satvik Dan*. On the other hand, that Dan which is given with a hope of getting something back in return or which causes regret, post facto, is called Rajasik.

Tamasik Dan is that charity which is given with haughtiness and contempt to non-deserving candidates at an improper place and at an inopportune time.

What is coming out of all the above is that a devotion which is founded upon *Satvik guna* in all its aspects-worship, contemplation (*Tap* तप) and charity (*Dan* दान) is also capable of taking a person 'there'. Krishna says that *Brahman* is referred to as *Om, Tat* and *Sat*, 'ॐ तत् सत् इति निर्देशः'. Those who engage in Satvik worship, contemplation and charity with complete devotion and with *Om, Tat* and *Sat*, 'ॐ तत् सत्' in mind, they, too, will realize *Brahman*. Therefore, the rigour of *Yogic* processes is not the only path. The key point Krishna seems to be making here is that whether nature of *Atman* and *Brahman* is realized following a yogic process or by following the path of *Bhakti*, the spiritual seeker needs to transcend beyond the three *gunas*, which are an integral aspect of the nature of a person, all actions of person and of all interactions of person with one another and with the nature around a person.

Chapter-XVI
The Sixteenth Question of Arjun

अर्जुनस्य षोडश: प्रश्न:

संन्यासस्य महाबाहो तत्त्वम् इच्छामि वेदितुम्
त्यागस्य च हृषीकेश पृथक् केशिनिषूदन (१८:१)

"I would like to know the facts (तत्त्व) about the 'state of renunciation' (संन्यास) and also, separately, the facts about the 'act of renouncing' (त्याग)", asks Arjun in his last question. Krishna proposes the following as a definitional, starting point:

काम्यानां कर्मणां न्यासं संन्यासं कवय: विदु:
सर्वकर्मफल त्यागं प्राहु: त्यागं विचक्षणा: (१८:२)

Wise people (कवय:) define *Sanyas* as relinquishing of 'all worldly acts which result in an excessive attachment to their outcomes' (काम्यानां कर्मणां) and *Tyag* as 'relinquising of excessive attachment to outcomes' (सर्वकर्मफल त्यागं) of all worldy acts. Krishna further adds that, 'त्याज्यं दोषवत् इति एके कर्म प्राहु: मनीषिण:, यज्ञ दान तप: कर्म: न त्याज्यम् इति च अपरे (१८:३)', some thinkers are, also, of the opinion that all worldly acts should be avoided and, therefore, they are a good candidate for renouncing. On the other hand, some other thinkers say that *Yagya* (यज्ञ), *Dan* (दान) and *Tapasya* (तपस्या) are types of worldly acts which should not be relinquished. However, in Krishna's opinion:

यज्ञ दान तप: कर्म: न त्याज्यम् कार्यम् एव तत्
यज्ञ: दानम् तप: च एव पावनानि मनीषिणाम् (१८:५)

Yagya (यज्ञ), *Dan* (दान) and *Tapasya* (तपस्या) are desirable acts and they are, by their very nature, not to be relinquished. These have a 'cleansing' impact on thinkers' minds. All these acts should be performed without the ego of doer-ship and without excessive attachment to their outcome (एतानि अपि तु कर्माणि सङ्गं त्यक्त्वा फलानि च, कर्त्तव्यानि इति ....१८:६). The act of relinquishing, *Tyag* (त्याग), is also classified into three types, depending upon the reason for Tyag,- Tamasik, Rajasik and Satvik. If Tyag is done because of ignorance, *moh*, it is called Tamasik; if it is done due to a fear of physical pain, then, it is called Rajasik; and if it is done without the asciption of doer-ship and without excessive attachment to the outcome of one's actions, then, it is called Satvik. Krishna is being a realist when he says that it is not possible for a person in this world to relinquish all worldly actions. However, those who are not excessively attached to the fruits of their actions, they, truly, deserve to be called a *Tyagi*:

न हि देहभृता शक्यग त्यक्तुम् कर्माणि अशेषतः
यः तु कर्मफलत्यागी सः त्यागी इति अभिधियते (१८:११)

One is reminded of Krishna's earlier statement(2:47) :

कर्मणि एव अधिकारः ते मा फलेषु कदाचन
मा कर्मफल हेतुः भूः मा ते सङ्गः अस्तु अकर्मणि (२:४७)

"Arjun, do your professional duties (कर्म as contrasted with अकर्म and विकर्म). Do not get overly attached to the outcome of your duties. You must not ascribe the cause of your duties to yourself nor should you allow yourself to be beset with 'not doing your professional duties' (अकर्म)".

Incidently, this statement of Krishna is also one of the most often quoted statements and it seems appropriate to conclude Arjun-Krishna dialogue with this verse from the Gita.

ॐ तत् सत्

Chapter XVII
Maitreyi-Yagyavalkya Dialogue

मैत्रेयी-याज्ञवल्क्य संवाद

This dialogue takes place between a husband, Yagyavalkya, and his wife, Maitreyi in Brihad-Aranyak Upanishad. Besides being a normal householder, Yagyavalkya was also a great spiritual teacher of his times. When one goes through the Sanskrit literature, one finds that it is very likely that several other teachers have also called themselves Yagyavalkya (याज्ञवल्क्य), because his name appears in many spiritual dialogues across several centuries. The context for this dialogue is the time when Yagyavalkya is ready to leave his duties as a householder and go to the forest to spend the third and the fourth stages of his life, called *Vanprastha* and *Sanyas*, respectively, there. He speaks with Maitreyi (मैत्रेयी) and tells her about his desire to renounce worldly attachments and and about his plans to go to the forest. Before he executes his plan, he wants to divide his worldly possessions between his two wives- Maitreyi (मैत्रेयी), his intellectual companion, and Gargi Katyayani (गार्गी कात्यायनी), who was his wife as a householder. Upon hearing her husband's plans, Maitreyi asks him a question, "What will I do with that wealth by which I won't become immortal?" Upon being inspired thus, Yagyavalkya, then, takes his wife, Maitreyi, on her own unique spiritual journey.

Yagyavalkya (याज्ञवल्क्य) says, "Maitreyi, I am about to depart for the forest and take leave from the life of a householder. Let me make a final settlement between you and

Katyayani for all the material possessions". (मैत्रेयी इति ह उवाच याज्ञवल्क्य उद यास्यन् वा अरे अहम् अस्मात् स्थानात् अस्मि, हन्त ते अनया कात्यायन्याऽन्तम् करवाण इति)

Maitreyi responds thus, "If all the wealth on this earth were mine, will I become immortal by having that?" (सा ह उवाच मैत्रेयी यत् नु म इयम् भगोः सर्वा पृथिवई वित्तेन पूर्णा स्यात् कथं तेन अमृता स्याम् इति)

"No, you will be leading a wealthy life like other wealthy people. However, you will not attain immortality only by possessing wealth". (न इति ह उवाच याज्ञवल्क्यः यथा एव उपकरणवतां जीवितम् तथा एव ते जीवितम् । स्यात् अमृतत्वस्य तु नाशास्ति वित्तेन इति)

Maitreyi asked, "Then, what will I do with that through which I will not become immortal? Tell me the way, instead, to become immortal". (सा ह उवाच मैत्रेयी येन अहम् न अमृता स्याम् किम् अहम् तेन कुर्याम् यद एव भगवान् वेद तद एव मे ब्रूहीति)

Yagyavalkya said, "O dear, you are speaking words which are close to my heart and you have spoken such words before. Come, sit down. I will explain to you. And when I am explaining to you, I am asking you to reflect on what I say". (स ह उवाच याज्ञवल्क्यः प्रिया बत अरे नः सती प्रियम् भाषसे एहि आस्स्व। व्याख्यास्यामि ते व्याचक्षाणस्य तु मे निदिध्यासस्व इति)

After asking Maitreyi to 'reflect on what I say', Yagyavalkya starts the spiritual journey with Maitreyi thus, "A husband is dear to the wife not for the sake of the husband but for the sake of *Atman*; not for the sake of the wife, a wife is dear to the husband but for the sake of *Atman*; not for the sake of the children are children dear to the parents but for the sake of the

Atman; not for the sake of the wealth is wealth dear to the rich but for the sake of the *Atman*; not for the sake of brahminhood is brahminhood dear but for the sake of the *Atman*; not for the sake of *kshatriyahood* is *kshatriyahood* dear but for the sake of the *Atman*; not for the sake of the world, around us, the world is dear but for the sake of *Atman*." And furthermore, he says, "Not for the sake of the gods are the gods dear but for the sake of the *Atman*; not for the sake of the beings are the beings dear but for the sake of the *Atman*; not for the sake of all is all dear but for the sake of the *Atman*."

Yagyavalkya summarizes this, for Maitreyi, by saying, "O Maitreyi, it is the *Atman* that should be seen, heard of, reflected upon and understood. Verily, by the seeing of, by the hearing of, by reflecting upon and by the understanding of Atman, all is known" (मैत्रेयी, आत्मनो वा अरे दर्शनेन श्रवणेन मत्या विज्ञानेन इदम् सर्वम् विदितम्). Yagyavalkya further emphasizes the centrality of the Atman as follows, "A Brahmin ignores one who knows him different from the Atman; the Kshatriya ignores one who knows him different from the Atman; the worlds ignore one who knows the worlds different from the Atman; the gods ignore one who knows them different from the Atman.......... All ignore one who knows it different from the Atman. This Brahmin, this Kshatriya, these worlds, these gods, these beings and this, all, are this *Atman* (इदम् ब्रह्म, इदम् क्षत्रम्, इमे लोकाः, इमे देवाः, इमानि भूतानि, इदम् सर्वम् यद अयम् आत्मा)". Yagyavalkya, after asserting that 'all this is nothing but Atman, the Self', now, moves on to unite all this by affirming that all this consists of nothing but knowledge:

"As the ocean is the uniting place for all waters, as the skin is by which all touch is felt, as the nostrils are the place where all smell is felt, as the tongue is the place for all tastes, as the forms are felt by the eyes, as the ears hear all the sounds, as the mind is the instrument for all determinations…………… and as the speech unites all knowledge. As a lump of salt thrown in water becomes dissolved in water and it cannot be seized forth as it were before dissolution, however, wherever one may take, it is salty indeed. So, verily, 'this great being, infinite and limitless, consists of nothing but knowledge' (इदम् महत् भूतम् अनन्तम् अपारम् विज्ञानघन एव). Yagyavalkya further adds, "Arising from out of these elements, one vanishes away into them. When one has departed, there is no more knowledge, this is what I say, my dear (एतेभ्यः भूतेभ्यः समुत्थाय तानि एव अनुविनश्यति, न प्रेत्य संज्ञा अस्ति इति अरे)". Maitreyi, who has been listening to and reflecting upon what Yagyavalkya has been saying all this time, makes a comment now.

Maitreyi says, "You have indeed confused me by saying that when one has departed, there is no more knowledge (न प्रेत्य संज्ञा अस्ति)".

On this, Yagyavalkya says, "Certainly, I have not said anything which can cause confusion. This should be enough for knowledge"(and, thus, enough for an answer to the question Maitreyi had asked in the beginning). It appears that Yagyavalkya has issued sort of a warning shot, by saying 'this should be enough for knowledge' and that his spiritual discourse is about to come to a close. However, he tries to explain further:

"Where there is a relationship of inter-dependent duality like the one between the smell and the smeller, between the seen and the seer, between the taste and the taster, between the speech and the speaker, between the hearing and the word spoken, between the thought and the thinker and between the understanding and that which is being understood, now, when everything has become *Atman*, then by what and by whom one should smell, then by what and whom should one see, then by what and whom should one hear, then by what and to whom one should speak, then by what and on whom should one think, then by what and whom should one understand? By what should one know that by which all this is known (येन इदम् सर्वम् विजानाति तम् केन विजानीयात्)? By what, my dear, one should know the knower (विज्ञातारम् अरे केन विजानीयात्)?" Yagyavalkya thus concludes his response to an apparently simple question from Miatreyi, 'If all the wealth on this earth were mine, will I become immortal by having that?'. His question is:

'By what, my dear, one should know the knower (विज्ञातारम् अरे केन विजानीयात्)?'

'Now, when everything has become *Atman*, then by what and by whom one should smell...... then by what and whom should one see..... then by what and to whom one should speak....... then by what and on whom should one think, then by what and whom should one understand...... by what should one know that by which all this is known'? This reminds one, indeed, of the state when there is no verb between the seer and the seen, between the hearer and the heard. This is, indeed, the dream of a *sufi*, the dream of a *qawwal*, the dream of a *ghazal* singer and the dream of a *Nirguna* singer. Realizing oneself is realizing god, indeed.

Now, it is also clearer why Krishna wanted Arjun to understand *Atman*.

Chapter-XVIII
Yama-Nachiketa Dialogue

यम-नचिकेता संवाद

This dialogue, between Yama and Nachiketa, has been taken from *Kath Upanishad*, which belongs to the *Taitariya* school of *Yajur Ved*. The story of Yama and Nachiketa has been, for the first time, mentioned as early as in the Rig Ved (10:135) itself. The background in which Nachiketa goes to meet Yama is an interesting one. Vajashravas (वाजश्रवस), who is also known as Uddalak (उद्दालक) *rishi*, Nachiketa's father, was giving away old and weak cows as gifts (दक्षिणा) to the priests who had participated in a *yagya* organized by him. He, out of his parental affection and attachment for Nachiketa, had kept some young and healthy cows for his son. Nachiketa found this out and went to his father offering himself to be given to a priest. Nachiketa understood the meaninglessness behind his father organizing a big *yagya* and, then, giving away old and weak cows as gifts. He goes to his father and asks, "To whom will you give me?" Upon noticing a complete silence from his father, he repeated this question a second time and a third time. Vajashravas, after sufficiently feeling irritated, said in anger, "To Death I shall give you (मृत्यवे त्वा ददामि)".

Nachiketa had thought that if his father would give him away, then, there would not be a need for his father to keep healthy and young cows for his son and, thus, his father would be saved from the bane of giving away old and weak cows to priests.

Nachiketa makes a farewell statement to his father, "अनुपश्य यथा पूर्वे प्रतिपश्य तथा अपरे, सस्यम् इव मर्त्यः पच्यते

सस्यम् इव अजायते पुनः (१:१:६)", 'Father, please look at the examples set by your ancestors and other great people of the past and present. They always followed up on what they said. You, too, should follow up on what you have said, implying that his father should not stop him from going to Death. In this world, whoever is born will die, one day, just like the rice plant which grows, gets old and, then, withers away (सस्यम् इव मर्त्यः पच्यते सस्यम् इव अजायते पुनः)'. Nachiketa left for Yama's abode.

Nachiketa reached Yama's place but did not find him there. Yama's wife offered him water and meal but he refused to partake of that. After three days when Yama came back to his house, his wife narrated the story of Nachiketa's refusal to eat. Yama, after hearing this story, asked Nachiketa to ask him for three boons (वर), one each for each night he spent without eating. As a first boon, Nachiketa asks Yama to make sure that his father does not get overly worried because his son has gone to Yama and that his father's anger calms down when Nachiketa returns home.   As a second boon, Nachiketa asks Yama to tell him about the *Agni* which is a means to go to Swarg, a place where,

स्वर्ग लोके न भयं किं च नास्ति, न तत्र त्वं न जरया विभेति
उभे तीर्त्वा अशनाया अपिपासे, शोकातिगः मोदते स्वर्ग लोके (१:१:१२)

there is no fear, no old age, no death, no hunger, no thirst, no sorrow and where there is nothing but bliss. Yama grants this wish by describing the means to go to Swarg. He goes a mile further by adding that this *Agni* will be known by his name, Nachiketa *Agni*, from now on. Yama, now, says, "Nachiketa, ask the third boon (तृतीयं वरं नचिकेतो वृणीष्व, १:१:२०)".

Nachiketa responds by saying that 'in some people's opinion, *Atman* survives after the death of this body. On the other hand, some say that nothing survives after death, i.e., there is no existence of *Atman* independent of this body. I would like to learn from you about what actually happens?' This was the third boon and, perhaps, the most complex one ,which Nachiketa had asked.

Upon hearing this, Yama said, "Nachiketa, this is a subtle and very difficult topic. Even in ancient times, many thinkers and philosophers have tried to answer this. But I am not sure whether they reached at a definite conclusion on this or not. Please ask me any other boon, instead (अन्यं वरं नचिकेतो वृणीष्व, १:१:२१)".

Nachiketa says, "Since you said that this is a subtle and very difficult topic and, even in ancient times, many thinkers and philosophers have failed to reach a definite conclusion about this, it must be a very important topic, worth knowing about. There is no other boon worth asking which is better than this (न अन्यः वरः तुल्यः एतस्य कश्चित, १:१:२२)".

Upon hearing this, Yama tries to pursuade Nachiketa by listing worldly things he could ask for as a boon-like great palaces, several hundred children, great wealth, horses, chariots, lots of land and fullfilment of all his material desires. Nachiketa remained steadfast and he said,

न वित्तेन तर्पणीयः मनुष्यः, लप्स्यामहे वित्तम् अद्राक्ष्म चेत् त्वा जीविष्यामः यावत् ईशिष्यसि त्वं, वरः तु वरणीयः सः एव (१:१:२७)

'Man can never be totally satisfied with wealth (न वित्तेन तर्पणीयः मनुष्यः)', Nachiketa argues, 'Just by visitng you, I have acquired lots of wealth and, furthermore, as long as you are the ruler of the world of the Dead, I hope to be alive, my life is guaranteed by your kingship. Therefore, the boon about the nature of *Atman* which I have asked for, earlier, is the one worthy of asking and nothing else'. Yama could not ignore this clever and powerful argument from Nachiketa and he embarked upon taking Nachiketa to a spiritual journey. Yama says (१:२:१),

अन्यत् श्रेय: अन्यत् उत एव प्रय:,
ते उभे नाना अर्थे पुरुषम् सिनीत:
तयो: श्रेय: आददानस्य साधु,
भवति हीयते अर्थात् उ प्रेय: वृणीते

There are two major different ways in this world-one is called the *Shreya* (श्रेय) path and the other is called *Preya* (प्रेय) path. People get attracted to both these paths, each having its own end-goal. But, generally speaking, *Shreya* (श्रेय) path takes a person to a higher goal, while the *Preya* (प्रेय) path takes a person to an end which should not be a desired goal of life. However, a person with a superior intellect chooses the *Shreya* (श्रेय) path, while one with an inferior intellect chooses the *Preya* (प्रेय) path, 'श्रेय: हि धीर: अभि प्रेयस: वृणीते, प्रेय: मन्द: योगक्षेमात् वृणीते (१:२:२)'. Yama throws light on some of the characteristics of a person who takes the *Preya* (प्रेय) path as follows (१:२:६),

न साम्पराय: प्रतिभाति बालं, प्रमाद्यन्तं वित्तमोहेन मूढम्
अयम् लोक: नास्ति पर: इति मानी, पुन: पुन: वशम् आपद्यते मे

"The follower of the *Preya* path, who has been blinded by wealth and material possessions, does not think that there is anything beyond what can be grasped with organs of sense perception. To that person, what is seen is the truth, what is heard is the truth, what is touched is the truth. A person, like this, dies again and again and comes to my kingdom several times". Earlier, Yama had tried to pursuade Nachiketa, by offering him a lot of material wealth, not to ask about *Atman*, but he had failed in his attempt. He has, now, determined that Nachiketa is on the *Shreya* (श्रेय) path and he is fully qualified to receive the knowledge about *Atman*, which Yama describes thus:

न जायते म्रियते वा विपश्चित् न अयम् कुतश्चित् न अयम् बभूव कश्चित्
अज:नित्य: शाश्वत: अयम् पुराण: न हन्यते हन्यमाने शरीरे (१:२:१८)

हन्ता चेत् मन्यते हन्तुम् हत: चेत् मन्यते हतम्
उभौ तौ न विजानीतो न अयम् हन्ति न हन्यते (१:२:१९)

This *Atman* neither gets born nor dies; it is neither born of anything/anyone nor begets anything/anyone(implying it is neither an effect nor a cause, principle of causality does not apply to *Atman*). It is unborn, eternal and indestructible. Those who think they killed someone and those who got killed consider themselves killed, they, both, do not know the true nature of *Atman*. Because, this *Atman* neither kills anyone nor gets killed by anyone. This is along the lines of what Krishna had told Arjun about the nature of *Atman*. So where does this *Atman* reside? How big is it, i.e., can it be measured? Yama continues,

अणो:अणीयान् महत: महीयान् आत्मा अस्य जन्तो: निहित: गुहायाम्
तं अक्रतु:पश्यति वीतशोक:धातुप्रसादात् महिमानम् आत्मन: (१:२:२०)

Somewhere, inside this 'body cave'(अस्य जन्तो: निहित: गुहायाम्), that *Atman* resides. It is smaller than the smallest and larger than the largest. Very rare people, with at least two qualities, *Nishkam* (निष्काम) and *Vitshok* (वीतशोक), are able to experience this *Atman*. Throwing light on the nature of *Atman*, Yama further adds this,

आसीनः दूरम् व्रजति शयानः याति सर्वतः
कः तम् मदामदम् देवं मत् अन्यः ज्ञातुं अर्हति (१:२:२१)

That remains still, however, that goes afar; that remains asleep, however, that goes everywhere. That *Atman* does not have a gross body, however, it resides in the gross body which is prone to change, 'अशरीरम् शरीरेषु अनवस्थेषु अवस्थितम्'. So how does one go about experiencing this *Atman*? Yama says, 'तस्य एषः आत्मा विवृणुते तनूम् स्वाम् (१:२:२३)', the perseverant seeker gets enlightened on its own by the nature of *Atman*. However, following the open-ended Vedic-Avesthic tradition, Yama tags his previous response by further saying, '*who can know where That is and in what form That is?*', कः इत्था वेद यत्र सः (१:२:२५)?

Moreover, the relationship between *Atman* and *Brahman* is similar to the one between the shadow and the light. *Atman* does not have an existence independent of the *Brahman*, 'छाया तपौ ब्रह्मविदः वदन्ति (१:३:१)'. Rigved describes this relationship between *Atman* and *Brahman* similarly:

द्वा सुपर्णा सयुजा सखाया समानं वृक्षं परिषस्वजाते
तयोःअन्यः पिप्पलं स्वाद्वत्त्यनश्नन् अन्यः अभिचाकशीति (१:१६४:१६)

Two beautiful birds are good friends and they reside on the same tree, the gross body form of an individual. However, one of them enjoys the sweet fruits of the tree, while the other looks on and is self-illuminated, that's how the Vedic rishi saw it. This is also similar to *Adhiyagya* and *Adhibhut* of

Krishna and *khodi* and *banda* of the Persian thinkers. Yama compares *Atman* as a passenger, this body as the chariot, wisdom as the charioteer, mind as the rein and sense-oragns as horses pulling the chariot. A wise charioteer always keeps the horses under one's control, an unwise one does not. It is very difficult to realize the true nature of *Atman* and *Brahman* if one's wisdom does not keep one's mind and, hence, ones sense organs, under control through the application of intellect, Yama says. This is similar to what Krishna had told Arjun and it is worth reproducing the pictorial model, first presented in Figure 2.1, as below:

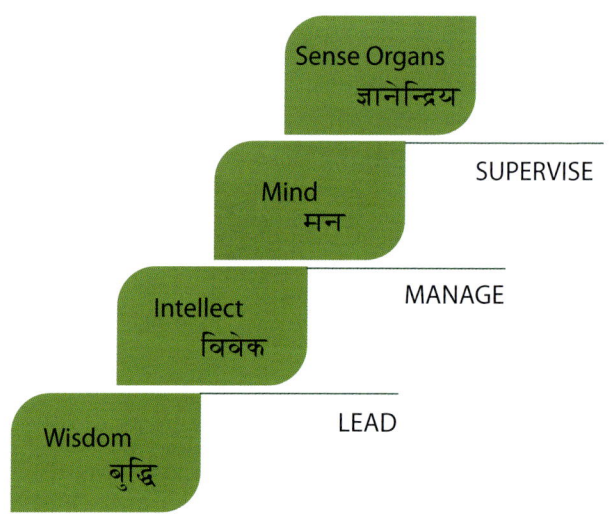

Figure 18.1

This is not a coincidence, because Bhagavad Gita's spiritual thoughts are rooted in Upanishadic thoughts. Yama also talks about the *Prakriti-Purush* model, also discussed in Arjun-Krishna dialogue, in detail, "महतः परं अव्यक्तम् अव्यक्तात् पुरुषः परः, पुरुषात् न परं किंचित् सा काष्ठा सा परा गतिः (१:३:११)", beyond the *Mahat Tatva*, is the unmanifested *Prakriti*, beyond that is the *Purush* and there is nothing beyond *Purush*. That is the ultimate end (सा काष्ठा सा परा गतिः). This knowledge can be realized by one with a subtle and sharp wisdom, "दृश्यते तु अग्र्यया बुद्धया सूक्ष्मया सूक्ष्मदर्शिभिः (१:३:१२)". After the nature of *Atman* and *Brahman* is realized, then, as Yama says (१:३:१५):

अशब्दम अस्पर्शम अव्ययम तथा अरसम नित्यम अगन्धवत च यत अनादि अनन्त महतः परं ध्रुवम् निच्चाय तं मृत्यु मुखात् प्रमुच्यते

"The true nature of *Atman* and *Brahman* is beyond the grasp of sensory organs, however, both are always there and both are indestructible, without beginning and without end. When one realizes this wisdom, then, one becomes immortal- one does not get born again and, therefore, does not die again (तं मृत्यु मुखात् प्रमुच्यते)."As one can see, Yama has not only shared with Nachiketa his ideas about the nature of *Atman* as Nachiketa had asked him for his third boon, but Yama has also asserted that one who understands the true nature of *Atman* becomes immortal, this is what Nachiketa had asked him as a part of his second wish.

Thus ends the Yama-Nachiketa dialogue.

Chapter-XIX
Narad-Sanatkumar Dialogue
नारद-सनत्कुमार संवाद

This dialogue, between Narad (नारद) and Sanatkumar (सनत्कुमार), has been taken from *Chhandogya Upanishad* which belongs to the *Sam Ved*. Narad, himself a great *rishi* of all times, goes to Sanatkumar, who was born of *Dharma* (धर्म) and *Ahimsa* (अहिंसा) as his father and mother, respectively. Sanatkumar has been depicted as an eternal five year old child in Indian spiritual books. Metaphorically, Sanatkumar is an eternal five year old child who is always curious, inquisitive and very wise. Narad asks him his first question, "Is there anything beyond the name(things with a name)? Tell that to me." Sanatkumar, in all his wisdom, shares his spiritual discovery with Narad and takes Narad, progressively, from the temporal to the time-transcendent; from what can be seen, heard, touched, tasted, smelled to that which is beyond all this- unseeable, un-hearable, un-touchable, un-tasteable and un-smellable, 'अशब्दम् अस्पर्शम् अव्ययम् तथा अरसम् नित्यम् अगन्धवत् च यत् अनादि अनन्त महतः परं ध्रुवम्', as Yama had described to Nachiketa. Narad, going closer to Sanatkumar said, "Teach me, venerable sir".

Sanatakumar said, "Tell me, first, what you know already. Then I will teach you what is beyond that".

Narad said, "I know the *Rig Ved*, the *Yajur Ved*, the *Sam Ved*, the *Atharv Ved*, the epics and the ancient stories, grammar, the science of numbers, the science of portents, the science of Time, logic, ethics, politics, the science of gods, ……. the science of weapons, astronomy and the fine arts. This much I know".

Narad continued, "But, sir, I am only like a person who knows the words and who is not a knower of *Atman*. It has been heard by me that he who knows *Atman* crosses over sorrow.......... Please help me to cross over the other side of sorrow".

Sanatkumar replied, "True, whatever you have learned is only a name. All this is mere name".

Narad asked, "Sir, is there anything beyond the name?"

Sanatkumar responded, "Yes, there is something beyond the name."

Narad eagerly asked, "Tell that to me, sir. (तत् मे ब्रवीतु इति)"

Sanatkumar said, "Speech is beyond the name, वाक् वा व नाम्नो भूयसी, because it is the speech which makes known all the topics you have learnt, as listed by you earlier. If there were no speech, neither right nor wrong would be known, neither the true nor the false, neither the good nor the bad, neither the pleasing nor the unpleasing. Speech, indeed, makes all this known. Contemplate on speech, therefore- वाचम् उपास्वेति".

Narad asked again, "Sir, is there anything beyond speech?"

Sanatkumar replied, "मनो वा व वाचो भूयः:, Mind is beyond speech. It is the mind which experiences (अनुभवति) speech and name. Mind, being the origin and experiencer of all, is indeed this *Atman*, mind is the world, mind is indeed *Brahman*. Contemplate on mind (मनःहि आत्मा मनः हि लोकः मनः हि ब्रह्म मनं उपास्वेति)".

Narad asked again, "Sir, is there anything beyond the mind?"

Sanatkumar replied, "Yes, there is something beyond the mind. It is called will (संकल्प), संकल्पः वा व मनसो भूयान. Because when one wills, then one reflects, then one utters speech and then one utters it in name. All these- mind, speech, name- are rooted in Will, have the Will as their innnermost resident and they, all, abide in Will. Therefore, contemplate on Will".

Narad raises another question, "Sir, is there anything beyond the Will?"

Sanatkumar replied, "Yes, there is something beyond the it- it is called thought (चित्त), चित्तम् वा व संकल्पाद् भूयः. Thought is certainly beyond Will, because when one thinks then one wills, then one reflects, then one speaks and one speaks it in name. All these center in thought, have thought as their goal and abide in thought. Therefore, even if a person has learnt a lot, but is unthinking, people call that person good for nothing, notwithstanding how much and whatever he may know. On the other hand, if one is thoughtful, even though one knows little, to him people are desirous of listening (तस्माद् यदि अपि बहुविद अचित्तः भवति, न अयम् अस्ति इति एव एनम् आहुः यद अयम् वेद, यद् वा अयम् विद्वान न इत्थम् अचित्तः स्यात् इति, अथ यदि अल्पविद चित्तवान भवति, तस्मा एवोत शुश्रूषन्ते ।) "

Narad's next question is, "Sir, is there anything beyond thought?"

Sanatkumar replied, "Yes, there is something beyond the thought- it is called contemplation (ध्यानम्), ध्यानम् वा व चित्ताद् भूयः, it is the concentration of all one's thoughts on one subject".

Sanatkumar progressively takes Narad, as he keeps asking what is beyond what has been said before, from a temporal view of one's self to a time-transcendent view. He successively says, understanding (विज्ञानम्) is beyond contemplation, strength (बलम्) is more important than understanding, food (अन्नम्) is important for strength, water (जलम्) is important for food, energy (तेज:) is required for water, space (आकाश) is beyond energy, memory (स्मर:) is beyond space, hope (आशा) is greater than memory, life-force (प्राणम्) is greater than hope. Sanatkumar pauses, at this point, by saying that *the life-force is all this* (प्राण: हि एव एतानि सर्वाणि भवति), implying that *if there is no life-force, then, all other things, said before, become irrelevant.*

At this point, Narad does not ask Sanatkumar whether there was something which was beyond the life-force. Sanatkumar, on his own, takes Narad to another plane- from an empirical world to a metaphysical one. He says, "One , truly, speaks excellently, who speaks excellently of truth." Narad replies, "But I, sir, would speak excellently of truth." Sanatkumar says, "But, one must desire to understand truth", thus planting a question in Narad's mind. Narad expresses his willingness to understand truth by saying, "Sir, I desire to understand the truth."

Sanatkumar says, "*Truly, when one understands, then, one speaks the truth. One who does not understand does not speak the truth. Only he, who understands, speaks the truth* (विजानन्न एव सत्यम् वदति). *Therefore, one must desire to understand understanding.*"

Narad says, "Sir, I desire to understand understanding."

Sanatakumar responds, "*Truly, when one thinks, then one understands. One who does not think does not understand. One who thinks understands. Then, one must desire to understand thinking*".

Narad promptly says, "Sir, I desire to understand thinking".

Sanatkumar continues to successively list *Shraddha*(devotion), *Nishtha*(steadfastness), *Kriti*(activity) and *Sukham*(happiness).

'And what is happiness?', Narad asks one more question.

Sanatkumar says, "*The infinite is happiness* (य: वै भूमा तत् सुखम्), *there is no happiness in anything which is finite. Then, one must desire to understand the Infinite.*"

Narad said, "Sir, I desire to understand the Infinite".

Sanatkumar responds thus, "*When one sees nothing, hears nothing, understands nothing, that is the Infinite….. verily, the Infinite is the same as immortal, the finite is the same as the mortal. The Infinite is below, it is above, it is behind, it is in front, it is in the south, it is in the north. It is indeed all this. And so is Atman, from where the Life-force springs forth, everywhere and everything- all this world* (अहम् एव इदम् सर्वम् इति). *One who sees this does not see death nor illness nor any sorrow.*" In his own words,

न पश्यो मृत्युम् पश्यति न रोगम् नोत दुःखताम्
सर्वम् ह पश्य: पश्यति सर्वम् आप्नोति सर्वश:

Sanatkumar's response to Narad's request, 'Sir, I desire to understand the Infinite', goes like this, "When one sees nothing, hears nothing, understands nothing, that is the Infinite….. verily, the Infinite is the same as immortal, the finite is the same as the mortal. The Infinite is below, it is above, it is behind, it is in front, it is in the south, it is in the north. It is indeed all this. And so is *Atman*, from where the life-force springs forth, everywhere and everything- all this world (अहम् एव इदम् सर्वम् इति)". This is very simliar to the spiritual model of a person as depicted in Figure 1.0 and reproduced.

Atman is at the core of a person. After all interactions with the external world are suspended and all internal thoughts

A Spiritual Model of a Person
Figure 19.1

are arrested at a standstill, then, what is left and felt is *Atman* which is everywhere and everything- all this world (अहम् एव इदम् सर्वम् इति)". *This is the extension of the Infinite, resident in the temporal Finite.* Yagyavalkya had also asserted this to Maitreyi, "This Brahmin, this Kshatriya, these worlds, these gods, these beings and this, all, are this Atman (इदम् ब्रह्म, इदम् क्षत्रम्, इमे लोका:, इमे देवा:, इमानि भूतानि, इदम् सर्वम् यद अयम् आत्मा)". Yama had told Nachiketa, "That *Atman* does not have a gross body, however, it resides in the gross body, which is prone to change, 'अशरीरम् शरीरेषु अनवस्थेषु अवस्थितम्'. So how does one go about experiencing this *Atman*? Yama had said to Nachiketa, 'तस्य एष: आत्मा विवृणुते तनूम् स्वाम् (१:२:२३)', *the perseverant seeker gets enlightened on its own by the nature of Atman*".

Chapter-XX
Balaki-Ajatshatru Dialogue

बालाकि-अजातशत्रु संवाद

Ajatshatru was the king of Kashi, the modern day Varanasi in India, which is one of the seven sacred places along with Ayodhya, Mathura, Kanchi, Avantika, Puri and Dvarvati. Dript Balaki belonged to the Gargya genealogy and was an expositor (वक्ता, अनुचानः). Even though he was a Brahmin, literally meaning one who knows *Brahman* (ब्रह्मम् अणाति इति ब्राह्मणः), he had an imperfect knowledge of *Brahman* (वृह्मन्), while Ajatshatru, despite being a king and a Kshatriya, is said to have an advanced knowledge of *Brahman*. This dialogue evolves, progressively, to a higher understanding of *Brahman* and is taken from Brihad-Aranyak Upanishad.

Balaki approached Ajatshatru and, boastingly, offered, "I will tell you about *Brahman* (ब्रह्मा ते ब्रवाणीति)."

Ajatshatru replied, "For this, I will give you a gift of thousand cows".

Balaki said, "That which is far away in the Sun, I meditate upon him as the *Brahman* (यः एवासाव आदित्ये पुरुषः, एतम् एव अहम् ब्रह्मोपास इति)"

Ajastshatru responded to this claim, "Please do not talk to me about this (मा मैतस्मिन संवदिष्ठा). I meditate on him as the one who is beyond everything and who is the head and the ruler of all beings. He who meditates on him as such also goes beyond everything".

Balaki said, "That which is far away in the Moon, I meditate upon him as the *Brahman* (यः एवासाव चन्द्रे पुरुषः, एतम् एव अहम् ब्रह्मोपास इति)"

Ajastshatru responded to this claim, "Please do not talk to me about this (मा मैतस्मिन संवदिष्ठा). I meditate on him as the great white-robed *Soma*. He who meditates on him as such, for him, Soma is poured out every day. His food never runs out (न अस्य अन्नम् क्षीयते)".

Balaki said again, "That which is far away in the Lightening, on him, indeed, I meditate as the *Brahman* (यः एवासाव विद्युति पुरुषः, एतम् एव अहम् ब्रह्मोपास इति)"

Ajastshatru responded to this new claim, "Please do not talk to me about this (मा मैतस्मिन संवदिष्ठा). I meditate on him as the radiant. He who meditates on him as such also becomes radiant and his offsprings, too, become radiant".

Balaki, then, successively talks about meditating on *Akash*(sky), on *Vayu*(air), on *Agni*(Fire), on *Ap*(water), on *Adarsh*(reflecting surface, mirror), on *Shabda*(sound), on *Disha*(direction), on *Chhayamaya*, person having a shadow, and , then, he says, "I meditate on That which is inside".

Upon this, Ajatshatru says, "Is that all?"

Balaki replies, "That is all".

Ajatshatru said, "With only that much, That is not known (नैतावता विदितम् भवति)". Balaki hurriedly said, "Let me come to you as a student, then".

Both got up and walked up to a person who was asleep. They both greeted him but he did not get up. Ajatshatru, then, woke him up by rubbing him with his hand. Ajatshatru asked Balaki, "Where was this person's intelligence when he was asleep and whence did it come back?" Balaki did not answer as he did not know. Ajatshatru said, "When this person, who possesses intelligence, fell asleep thus, having by his intelligence taken to himself the intelligence of his sense organs, he rests in the space within his heart. When a person 'takes in' his senses, he is said to be asleep. When the breath is restrained, the eyes are restrained, the ears are restrained, the speech is restrained and the mind is restrained (गृहीतम् मनः)".

Ajatshatru further continued, "When one falls sound asleep, when he knows nothing whatsoever, having come through the seventy two thousand channels, called *hita* (हिता), which extend from the heart to the pericardium, he rests in the pericardium, as if he has reached the summit of bliss. As a spider moves along the threads, as small sparks come forth from fire, similarly, from this *Atman* come forth all breaths, all worlds and all beings. *Its deep meaning is the truth of truth. Vital breaths are the truth and their truth is That, the Atman* (सत्यस्य सत्यम् इति, प्राणा वै सत्यम्, तेषाम् एष सत्यम्)!"

Sanatkumar had also asserted this to Narad, "..... *Atman*, which is everywhere and everything- all this world (अहम् एव इदम् सर्वम् इति)". This is the extension of the Infinite, resident in the temporal Finite. This is the *Adhiyagya* as described by Krishna to Arjun. This is the *khodi*, the *roh* of the Persians.

Chapter-XXI
Valikhilya-Prajapati Dialogue

वालिखिल्य-प्रजापति संवाद

This dialogue, between Valikhilyas and Prajapati, was narrated by *rishi* Shakayanya (शाकायन्य) to king Brihadrath (बृहदरथ), who was a descendent of the king, Ikshvaku (ईक्ष्वाकु). This has been taken from *Maitri Upanishad*, which belongs to the *Maitrayaniya* branch of the Krishna Yajur Ved. *Rishi Maitri* was the founder of this branch of rishis to which Shakayanya belonged. The dialogue captures the spiritual quest of a king as Shakayanya tells Brihadrath, "Now, indeed, O King, this is the knowledge about *Brahman*…….as declared to us by revered Maitri……I will narrate it to you." Shakayanya, then, goes on narrating the dialogue between Valikhilyas and Prajapati as follows.

Valikhilayas said, "This body is like a cart without consciousness. Under whose invisible influence, this body acquires consciousness (भगवन्, शकटम् इव अचेतनम् इदम् शरीरम्, कस्य एष खलु इहृशः महिमा अतीन्द्रिय भूतस्य, येन एतद् विधं इदम् चेतनवत् प्रतिष्ठापितम्)? Whatever you know, tell us that."

Prajapati responded, "By That, which is beyond speech and hearing and which is pure, clean, void, tranquil, abiding in its own greatness, endless, indestructible, eternal, unborn and self-volitioned, this body acquires consciousness (यः ह खलु वाचोपरिस्थः श्रयते सः एव वा एष शुद्धः पूतः शून्यः शान्तः प्राणोऽनीशात्माः अनन्तः अक्षय्यः स्थिरः शाश्वतः अजः स्वतंत्रः स्वे महिम्नि तिष्ठति अनेन इदम् शरीरम् चेतनवत् प्रतिष्ठापितम्) .

Valikhilyas asked, "How is it possible that someone/something with aforementioned characteristics can bestow consciousness in this body?"

Prajapati replied, "Truly, that subtle, ungraspable and invisible *Purush* resides in this body with a part of himself which possesses an extension of its self-volition. This is very similar to a person waking up, out of one's own volition, from a deep sleep. That part of the *Purush* which is its own extension in every being is the *Kshetragya*, *which has characteristics of will, determination and self-reflection.* That is the one which is the mover behind this body." Krishna did also throw a lot of light on *Kshetragya* in his dialogues with Arjun. Briefly, *Kshetragya* is the knower of the body, " क्षेत्रम् शरीरम् तद् अहम् अस्मि इति जानाति इति क्षेत्रज्ञः")

Valikhilyas, still not satisfied with the answer, asked Prajapati, "How is That the body's mover?"

Prajapati responds by initiating an elaborate explanation, hoping that Valikhilyas' inquisitiveness would be satisfied.

He says, "In the beginning, That was alone (प्रजापतिः वा एषः अग्रे अतिष्ठत्, सः नार्मत एकः) . From its own volition, That constructed all this and saw it all lifeless like a stone, without understanding, unmoving and without consciousness. That thought to itself, 'let me enter within each of them in order to awaken them'. That became like a 'wind' and sought to enter them. Being one, That could not do it.

Therefore, That divided itself, first, fivefold into-*pran, apan, saman, udan and vyan,* the five types of breath-and, then, entered each of them.......That, after dividing itself fivefold, is hidden in a 'secret' place in each being and *That consists of mind, whose body is life, whose form is light, whose will is truth, whose Atman is space….* That was still not satisfied and, then, That said, 'Let me enjoy objects'……then, these sense organs were constructed…… which are like horses and this body is like a chariot and mind is the charioteer, by whom thus driven, this body moves around like the potter moving the pottery wheel….so this body is set up possessing consciousness and intelligence."

Prajapati continued, "Truly, this *Atman*, the *rishis* say, wanders here on earth in every being unaffected by the outcomes of one's *Karma-* good or bad. *Atman, being subtle, formless, imperceptible, ungraspable and free from self-sense, is a 'doer' only in appearance* (स: वा एष: आत्मा…… प्रतिशरीरेषु चरति अव्यक्तत्वात् सूक्ष्मत्वात् अदृश्यत्वात् अगाह्यत्वात् निर्ममत्वात् च अनवस्थ: अकर्ता कर्ता इव अवस्थित:). *Truly, that Atman is pure, steadfast, unmoving, unattached to the fruits of one's Karma, free from desire, steadfast and 'lives in itself', veiled by the three gunas- Satvik, Rajasik and Tamasik* (चरति भुक् गुणमयेन पटेन आत्मानम् अन्तर्धीय अवस्थित:)."

Valikhilyas heard Prajapati's monologue patiently, then, they asked another question, "Sir, we understand the characteristics of the *Atman* which remains unaffected by the evolutes of one's Karma- good or bad. Some people also talk about another *Atman* which gets affected by the evolutes of one's Karma. What is that one?" Basically what Valikhilyas want to know is whether there is a temporal complement of the time-transcedent *Atman* or not.

Prajapati responds again enthusiastically, "Yes, there is one beside *Atman*. That is called *Bhut-Atma* (अस्ति खलु अन्य: अपर: भूतात्मा…). And this is the way it is described. The combination of five *tanmatras*(*Shabda, Sparsh, Rup, Ras and Gandh*) and the five *maha-bhuts*(*Akash, Vayu, Agni, Ap and*

Prithvi) is called body. That which is limited to this aspect of the body is called the *Bhut-Atma*", which is the temporal equivalent of the time-transcedent *Atman* as described earlier. This *Bhut-Atma* is the one which gets affected by the good or the bad evolutes of one's Karma. Prajapati's *Atman*, thus, is Krishna's *Adhiyagya* and Prajapati's *Bhut-Atma* is Krishna's *Adhibhut*.

This *Bhut-Atma*, as Prajapati explains further, is the one which gets confused, gets 'tied' down by the three *gunas* in *Karma-Bandhans*. It is always moving, full of desire, distracted and under the influence of bad aspects of one's ego and id. *This very Bhut-Atma is the one which thinks, 'I am that, this is mine....' and binds itself with itself like a bird entangled in a bird-snare.* This is also that bird which, metaphorically, has been described in Shwetashwatar Upanishad (श्वेताश्वतर उपनिषद), as the bird which enjoys the fruits of its actions while the other one, the Atman, looks on dispassionately:

द्वा सुपर्णा सयुजा सखाय समानं वृक्षं परिषष्वजाते
तयोः अन्यः पिप्पलं स्वाद्वत्ति अनश्नन् अन्यः अभिचाकशीति (८:६)

Prajapati describes the *Atman* differently but lucidly, 'अथ अमृतः अस्य आत्मा बिन्दुः इव पुष्करा इति', *the time-transcendent Atman's relationship with the temporal body is like that between a drop of water on the lotus leaf*(a drop of water does not wet the lotus leaf).

Prajapati further adds that this body is an outcome of sexual intercourse, grows in the darkness of the womb, then, it comes forth through the urinary passage (शरीरम् इदम् मैथुनाद् इवोद्भतम् संविदपेतम् निरय एव मूत्रद्वारेण निष्क्रान्तम्). It is built up with bones covered with flesh and skin..... filled with faeces, urine, bile, phlegm, marrow, fat, grease and, also, many diseases…...

"It has been also said that confusion, fear, depression, excessive sleepiness, sloth, attention-defficiency, old age, hunger, weakness, anger, ignorance, jealousy, cruelty, stupidity, shamelessness, meanness and rashness are some of the characteristics of manifestation of forces of darkness. While, inner quest, affection, passion, hurting others, lust, hatred, deceit, enevy, insatiability, fickleness, excessive acquisitiveness, over-attachment to objects of pleasure etc. are some of the examples of the characteristics of the forces of passion. The *Bhut-Atma*, the Adhibhut, gets affected by all these forces and, therefore, the *Bhut-Atma* acquires many forms", says Prajapati.

Valikhilyas were very pleased with what they heard so far and they asked, once again, "What is the process by which this *Bhut-Atma*, after leaving this Time-bound body, unites with the Time-Transcendent *Atman* (अस्य कः विधिः भूतात्मनः येन इदम् हित्वात्मनि इव सायुज्यम् उपैति तान् ह उवाच)?"

Prajapati says, "Like the waves, in large rivers, there is no turning back of that which has been done previously (महानदीषु उर्मय इव निवर्तकम् अस्य यत् पुरा कृतम्)…….. like the tide of the ocean, the approach of one's death is hard to keep back……
like the one beset with delusion….. bitten by the objects of sense, like gross darkness, the darkness of passion, like jugglery consisting of illusion, like a dream, false appearances, like the inside of a banana tree, unsubstantial…… like a painted scene, falsely delighting the mind and therefore, it has been said, 'objects of sound, touch, taste and the like are worthless objects for man.. The *Bhut-Atma*, through attachment to them, does not remember the highest state."

Prajapati continues, "Acquisition of knowledge and performance of one's duty, dispassionately, consistent with the stage in one's life, indeed, are the antidote to this *Bhut-Atma's* illusion. One should also keep an eye, through *Tapasya* and meditation, on *Brahman*.

Valikhilyas exclaimed, "Sir, you are the teacher, you are the teacher. Whatever you have said has entered our minds. Now, answer one more question: *Agni, Vayu, Mitra, Yama, whatever it is, Pran, Annam Brahma, Rudra, Vishnu, some meditate upon one, some upon another. Tell us which one is better for us.*

Prajapati responded, "*These are but some of the forms of the immortal, the formless Brahman. To whichever one a person is devoted, in this world that person rejoices* (लोके प्रतिमोदति). *For it has been said, 'Truly, the whole world is Brahman* (ब्रह्म खल्तु व इदम् वा व सर्वम्)'. *And when all things perish, that person attains unity with Brahman*".

This ends the dialogue between Valikhilyas and Prajapati.

Chapter-XXII
Gargi-Yagyavalkya Dialogue

गार्गी- याज्ञवल्क्य संवाद

This dialogue takes place at a meeting of several *rishis* where Yagyavalkya is the chief guest. The meeting place is an *ashram* somewhere in the *Brihad Aranya*, literally the great forest and, thus, this dialogue has been taken from the Brihad-Aranyak Upanishad. Several *rishis* have already asked their questions and now it is the turn of Vachaknavi Gargi(different from Gargi, wife of Yagyavalkya), who gets up and addresses her peers, "Venerable Brahmins, I will ask him two questions. If he answers them both, then, none of you will succeed in defeating him in the debate about *Brahman*". Gargi's peers, in unison, said, "Ask them, Gargi".

Gargi turned to Yagyavalkya and said, "Yagyavalkya, that which is in the sky, that which is on the earth, that which is in between the earth and the sky and that which the people call the past, the present and the future, what all these are tied with?"

Yagyavalkya said, "That which is in the sky, that which is on the earth, that which is in between the earth and the sky and that which the people call the past, the present and the future, space are they tied with.

Gargi said to Yagyavalkya, "*Namaste*, Yagyavalkya. You have answered this question. Prepare for the next (अपर अस्मै धारयस्वेति)".

Yagyavalkya said, "Ask, Gargi".

Gargi asked, "Yagyavalkya, that which is in the sky, that which is on the earth, that which is in between the earth and the sky and that which the people call the past, the present and the future, what all these are ties with?" Gargi thus asked the same question again.

Unsurprisingly and, perhaps, teasingly, Yagyavalkya's answer was the same as before. Then, Gargi asked, "What is space tied with?"

This is a difficult question. Because, if Yagyavalkya does not answer this he is open to the charge of not understanding the question. If he answers, then, he would be guilty of contradiction by the virtue of explaining what, inherently, is inexplicable. However, Yagyavalkya, diplomatically, responds thus:

"O, Gargi, knowers of *Brahman* call that the imperishable. It is neither large nor small, neither short nor long, neither red nor adhesive. It is neither shadow nor darkness, neither air nor space, unattached, without taste, without smell, without sight, without hearing, without speech, without mind, without radiance, without breath, without a mouth, beyond measurement. *It has no within and no without* (अनन्तरम् अबाह्यम्). It consumes nothing and no one consumes it."

Yagyavalkya continues, "Because of its laws, the sun and the moon are situated where they are. Because of its laws, the sky and the earth are positioned where they are. O, Gargi, because of its laws, what are called moments, hours, days, nights, half-months, months, seasons and years happen. Because of its laws, some rivers flow to the East, while some flow to the West....... *Truly, O, Gargi, that Imperishable is unseen but is the seer, is unheard but is the hearer, is unthought but is the thinker, is unknown but is the knower. There is no other seer but this, there is no other hearer but this, there is no other thinker but this, there is no other knower but this.* With this Imperishable, this space is tied, O, Gargi." By saying this, it appears that Yagyavalkya hints towards gravity as the ultimate irreducible reality.

Upon hearing this, Gargi told his peers, "Respected Brahmins,….. not one of you will defeat him in arguments about *Brahman*".

Thereafter, Gargi kept silent.

Chapter-XXIII
Shakalya-Yagyavalkya Dialogue

शकल्य-याज्ञवल्क्य संवाद

The background for this dialogue is exactly the same as the one between Gargi and Yagyavalkya, same *ashram* in the same great forest and the same *rishis* gathered together to listen to and ask questions to Yagyavalkya. It is the turn of a *rishi* called Shakalya (शकल्य), who asked, "How many gods are there, Yagyavalkya?"

Yagyavalkya responded, "As many as are mentioned in the invocation of the gods, namely, three hundred and three, and three thousand and three."

Shakalya said, "Yes, but how many gods are there, Yagyavalkya?"

Yagyavalkya responded, "Thirty three."

Shakalya said again, "Yes, but how many gods are there, Yagyavalkya?"

Yagyavalkya responded, "Six."

Shakalya said again, "Yes, but how many gods are there, Yagyavalkya?"

Yagyavalkya responded, "Three."

Shakalya asked again, "Yes, but how many gods are there, Yagyavalkya?"

Yagyavalkya responded, "One and a half."

Shakalya asked again, "Yes, but how many gods are there, Yagyavalkya?"

Yagyavalkya responded, "One."

Shakalya took a sigh of relief and said, "Yes. But which are those three hundred and three and three thousand and three gods?"

Yagyavalkya responded, "They are but manifestations of them, but there are only thirty three gods."

Shakalya asked, "Which are these thirty three?

Yagyavalkya counted, "The eight *Vasus*, the eleven *Rudras*, the twelve *Adityas*, together, they total thirty one. Then Indra and Prajapati make up the other two. Thus, there are thirty three gods."

Shakalya asked again, "Which are the eight Vasus?"

Yagyavalkya enumerated, "*Agni, Prithvi, Vayu*, the *Sky*, all the Suns as one, Space, all the Moons as one and all planets together as one- these are eight Vasus."

Shakalya asked again, "Which are the Rudras?"

Yagyavalkya responded, "The ten breaths in a person and the mind make up the eleven Rudras. When they depart from this mortal body, they make us weep. Because they make us weep, they are called Rudras." As a side note, here the ten breaths imply the five sensory and the five motor organs in the body. Yagyavalkya, further, identifies the twelve Adityas with twelve months of the year and six gods with the four(Agni, Vayu, Prithvi and Akash) of the five *Maha-bhuts* and the sun and the space. To another question from Shakalya, "Which is the one god?"

Yagyavalkya said, "*Brahman*. They call him That(तत्)."

The dialogue between Shakalya and Yagyavalkya continues and expands to include more spiritual concepts which provides Shakalya a plural paltform for exploring his spirituality. Then, at the end, Shakalya asks him one more question, "Yagyavalkya, *in what you and your Atman are resident* (कस्मिन् नु त्वम् च आत्मा च प्रतिष्ठितौ स्थ इति)?" Yagyavalkya said, "In the *Pran* (प्राण), the life-breath, the inbreath, which is, in turn, supported by *Apan* (अपान), the outbreath, which is, in turn, supported by *Vyan* (व्यान), the diffused breath, and which is, in turn, supported by *Saman* (समान), the middle breath".

After this, Yagyavalkya hurriedly adds, "*But, that Atman is not this, not this* (स एष न इति, न इति आत्मा). *That is incomprehensible because it is not comprehended. It is indestructible because it is never destroyed..... it is free, it does not suffer.....it is not injured.* ".

Chapter-XXIV
Satyakam-Gautam Dialogue

सत्यकाम-गौतम संवाद

This dialogue has been taken from the Chhandogya Upanishad and captures the spiritual quest of Satyakam (सत्यकाम), a man of a very humble beginning and upbringing, with the help from Gautam (गौतम), a *rishi* and the son of Haridrumat (this Gautam is not the same as Gautam, the Buddha). Actually, a large part of this dialogue takes place between Satyakam and Agni and several animals including a cow-bull, named, *Rishabh*. Satyakam, filled with a strong desire for understanding the nature of the ultimate reality, went to his mother, Jabala (जबाला) and asked her, "Mother, I want to live a life of a *Brahmachari*, a student seeking spiritual knowledge. Of what family tree, of what *gotra*, am I from?"

Jabala replied, "My child, I do not know of what family tree you are from. During my youth, when I went around a great deal as a house maid, I conceived you. So I do not know what genealogy you belong to. However, my name is Jabala and you are called Satyakam. So you can call yourself Satyakam Jabal (सत्यकाम जाबाल). Satyakam, thus, got a last name, Jabal(जाबाल), son of Jabala (जबाला), and departed for *rishi* Gautam's *ashram*. He said to Gautam, "I wish to become a student of spiritual knowledge. May I become your student, sir?"

Gautam asked him, "Of what family tree are you, noble one?"

Satyakam replied, "I do not know this, sir. Before I came here, I asked my mother. She told me that during her youth, when she went around a great deal, as a house maid, she conceived me. So she did not know what family tree I came from. Howver, she gave me a family name- Jabal, and, I am now Satyakam Jabal."

Gautam said to Satyakam, "None other than a Brahmin could thus explain. Bring the fuel woods, noble one, I will have you as my student because you have not departed from the truth." Having initiated Satyakam into the ways of the *ashram*, Gautam separated four hundred skinny and weak cows and told Satyakam, "Go with these, noble one, and graze them." While going away, Satyakam said, "I may not return without a thousand." Thus, he lived away from the *ashram* for a number of years when the cows came to be a thousand.

Rishabh, a cow-bull, spoke thus, "Satyakam, we have reached a thousand, the noble one, take us to the *ashram*. And let me declare to you foundational columns (पाद) of *Brahman* (बृह्मन्)."

Satyakam replied, "Tell me, sir".

Rishabh spoke, "The East is one, the West is one, the South is one and the North is one . This is, truly, *Brahman's* four columned foundation, named *Prakashvan* (प्रकाशवान). He who, knowing this, meditates on this Prakashvan, also becomes Prakashvan. Agni will tell you about the other foundations of *Brahman.*"

Satyakam, then, started the journey to take the cows to the *ashram*. In the evening, he lit the fire, penned the cows and sat down to the west of the fire, facing the east. Agni called upon him, "Satyakam." Satyakam replied, "Respectable sir."

"Let me declare to you, noble one, a column of *Brahman. Prithvi*, the earth, is one, *Antariksha*, the horizon is one, *Dyau*, the space, is one and *Samudra*, the oceans, are one. This is Brahman's four-columned foundation, called the *Nantavan* (नान्तवान). He who, knowing this, meditates on this *Nantavan* (नान्तवान), also, becomes *Nantavan*. A swan will tell you another foundation."

Next day, again, on his way to the *ashram*, when Satyakam was resting in the evening, a swan told him, "Agni is one, the Mitra is one, the Soma is one and the lightening is one. This is *Brahman's* four-columned foundation, named *Jyotisman* (ज्योतिष्वान). A diver-bird will tell you another foundation of *Brahman*". And so it happened. A diver bird told Satyakam about another foundation of *Brahman* and, according to that, breath, eyes, ears and the mind made up the four foundational columns of *Brahman*, called *Ayatanavan* (आयतनवान)" . Next day, Satyakam arived at the *ashram*.

Gautam commented and asked Satyakam, "Noble one, you shine like the one as if you know *Brahman*. Who has taught you?"

Satyakam replied, "Others than men. But, I wish, sir, that you teach me. For, I have heard from persons like you, sir, that the knowledge which has been learnt from a teacher helps one the most to attain one's objectives."

Gautam, then, taught Satyakam- nothing was left out, yea, nothing was left out.

Chapter-XXV
Bhrigu-Varun Dialogue

भृगु-वरुण संवाद

This is a dialogue between a father, Varun (वरुण), and his son, Bhrigu (भृगु), and has been taken from *Taitariya Upanishad*, which belongs to the Taitariya school of *Yajur Ved*. The dialogue starts with a simple and candid question from the son to his father, "Sir, teach me about *Brahman* (अधीहि भगवो ब्रह्मा इति)."

Varun told him this, "Matter, life, sight, hearing, mind, speech (अन्नम् प्राणम् चक्षुश श्रोत्रम मनः वाचम् इति)." He further added, "*That, truly, from which these beings are born, that, by which, when born they live, that into which they dissolve. That, you should seek to know. That is Brahman.*" What Varun has told his son, Bhrigu, is about the model first shown in Figure 13.2 and reproduced above in Figure 25.1. There are three aspects of *Brahman- Ishnu, Vishnu* and *Grasishnu* (ईष्णुरु विष्णुरु ग्रसिष्णु) *each corresponding to (1) That, truly, from which these beings are born, (2) that, by which, when born they live, (3) that into which they dissolve.*

Bhrigu contemplated over what his father had said and he realized that the *matter is Brahman. Because, truly, beings are born from matter, they live by matter and into matter they enter upon departure.* After realizing this, he again approached his father and asked him, "Sir, teach me about *Brahman*". Varun told him to contemplate again and, after contemplating, Bhrigu reported to his father, "*Life is Brahman. For, beings are born from life, they live by life and into life they enter upon*

एक एव पर: विष्णु: सर्वत्र अपि न संशय

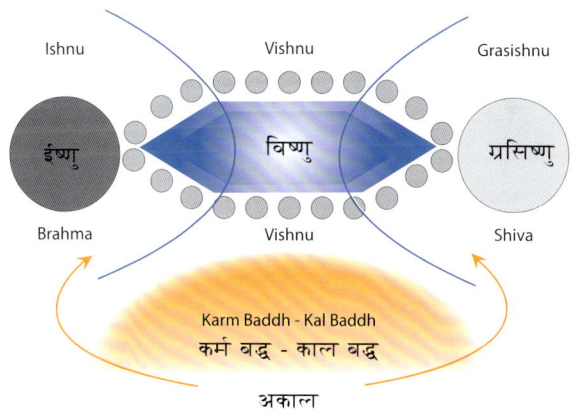

Figure 25.1

departure". Having said that, he again approached his father and said, "Sir, teach me about *Brahman*". Varun asked him to contemplate again.

Bhrigu realized thus, "*Mind is Brahman. For, beings are born from Mind, they live by Mind and into Mind they go upon departure*". Having said that, Bhrigu, again, approached his father and said, "Sir, teach me about *Brahman*". Varun asked him to contemplate again. Bhrigu contemplated and came to the conclusion that '*Intelligence is Brahman. For, beings are born from Intelligence, they live by Intelligence and into Intgelligence they go upon departure*'.

Thus, Bhrigu, progressively and successively, moved from a temporal plane to a non-temporal plane. Having realized that '*Intelligence is Brahman*', is not the final spiritual resting place, even though it is an important milestone along the process of seeking. Even intelligence has to be transcended. After this transcension beyond intelligence is achieved, then, a realization of the perfect bliss, *Ananda* (आनन्द), is attained. As philosopher Radhakrishnan puts it, "Intellectual man, who uses mind, life and body is greater than mind, life and body but he is not the end of cosmic evolution as he still has a secret aspiration. Even as matter contained life as its secret destiny and had to be delivered of it, life contained mind and mind contained intelligence and intelligence contains spirit(Atman) as its secret destiny and presses to be delivered of it. Intelligence does not exhaust the possibilities of consciousness and cannot be its highest expression….. *the crown of evolution is this deified consciousness*".

Bhrigu, truly, attained the crown of evolution, that 'deified consciousness', that *Ananda*, that perfect bliss as he tells his father, Varun, "*Bliss is Brahman. For, beings are born from bliss, they live by bliss and into bliss they go upon departure.*" Thus ended the dialogue between the father and the son.

Chapter-XXVI

foreword
प्राक्कथन

Why The Spirit Of One ?

During the last century, the world has gone through monumental changes. Such changes have largely been brought about by technological innovations which have enabled mankind to move away from a largely un-organized, agriculture-based economy to a well organized and well orchestrated bazaar-based economy. This shift in the mode of eking out a livelihood has, among other things, encouraged people to spend more time in the bazaar, marketing and selling their baskets of goods and services and negotiating and buying others' goods and services. This is in sharp contrast to the agriculture-based economic activities of the past when people used to spend more time at home and less time in the bazaar. The bazaar, in a sense, has become the home now. The activities in the bazaar leave little time to pause, to think and to reflect. Every part of the human body has become a target, an opportunity, for economic activities. Starting right from the hair on the head and down to the soles of a person's feet, several hundred thousand products and services have been innovated, globally, for a person to acquire and use. This broad spectrum of products and services, in modern times, has engendrered multiplicity of choices. The opportunity, most often guaranteed by governmental laws, to avail oneself of these choices is called the freedom of choice. Never before in human history has such a wide variety of choices been made available. The means to make a livelihood has multiplied by several orders of magnitude and each person, theoretically at least, is free to participate in the bazaar economy in the way a person chooses to. If a person, for example, does not succeed selling hair dye or a medicine for hair growth or a method for hair transplant, one might succeed by selling a lotion to keep the soles of the feet moist or by selling toiletry or sanitary towels. This is great because the bazaar economy has provided opportunities for making a decent and a civilized livelihood for scores of individuals.

However, at the same time, less and less choices are being made available in the spiritual realm of human existence. While the physical and the material environment of mankind offers several choices, the spiritual environment is being narrowed to offer fewer and fewer choices. A chasm has thus been created between the physical world of a person and the spiritual world of the person. This chasm is being, perhaps unintentionally, widened by some religious groups by their beliefs that their god is the only god and that, if one does not believe in their god, that person is condemned to go to hell and spend the after-life in a perpetual perdition. It is unfortunate that this license to limit spiritual choices of a person through 'freedom of religion' laws is not only being cherished by the modern world but is also being made a subtle condition for economic help to other unfortunate folks around the globe. These unforunate folks are called poor because they either do not feel a need for or have not figured out ways to design and develop thousands of products and services for each external as well as for some internal parts of the human body. They are placed low on economic indices due to a lack of an ownership of a large number of baskets of goods and services. Their misfortune is further compounded by the fact that they have a different god or gods. Religious commands like 'Thou shalt have none other gods before me…' are being made out to be a virtue and are being supported by enactment of and demand for laws guaranteeing 'freedom of religion'. It is, indeed, hard to imagine a better and a more visible contradiction than the one which exists between the religious commandments which say 'thou shalt have none other gods before me…' and 'freedom of religion' laws professed, propagated and demanded by several governments in the world today. Not only this, religious leaders who work tirelessly and relentlessly towards narrowing the spiritual choices of mankind are being rewarded and beatified as saints. We are indeed living in interesting times. Obvious and serious contradictions like this and the spiritual robbery of humanity do not seem to bother many anymore.

A question arises as to how long mankind will tolerate and live with such grave contradictions between the physical world and the spiritual world; between physical wealth and spiritual deprivation. Another question can also be raised as to how wide the chasm, between the physical and the spiritual world of a person, will become before mankind will realize that the spiritual choices are as much important, if not more, as the physical choices; individual spirituality is as important, if not more, as individual wealth. When shall we reconcile the gap between the two freedoms, the physical and the spiritual as well? How shall we close the chasm between the two worlds? How shall we open and expand the inner mind of each person so that a spiritual experience, which would be unique to the person, could be felt?

A potential answer to these questions lies in laying out a set of repeatable spiritual processes and process steps which progressively move a person first to experience the core of the person and then to connect that individuated core with the undifferentiated cosmic core. Such a progressive journey to the core of a person might encourage one to move away from religious doctrines which limit the freedom of and the choice for a unique spiritual experience leading to the spiritual awakening of a person. 'The Spirit of One' has been written to make each person think, understand, look within and reflect and, perhaps, experience one's own unique spirituality without exclusionary and divisive preconditions such as 'thou shalt have none other gods before me'. In our own times, Dr. Deepak Chopra has done a commendable job in his book 'How To Know God' by laying out a process. Works like this are beginning to free the spirit of men and women in not only America but also the whole world.

As the philosopher, Dr. S. Radhakrishnan, has remarked in his commentary on Upanishads, "Intellectual man, who uses mind, life and body is greater than mind, life and body but he is not the end of the cosmic evolution as he still has a secret aspiration. Even as matter contained life as its secret destiny and had to be delivered of it, life contained mind and mind contained intelligence and intelligence contains spirit as its secret destiny and presses to be delivered of it". He further continues, "Intelligence does not exhaust the possibilities of consciousness and cannot be its highest expression…….. the crown of evolution is this deified consciousness". The Spirit of One may act as a catalyst for the quest which Radhakrishnan has called 'this deified consciousness', the crown of evolution.

It is a celebration of each person's unique god, which does not have to be in the likeness of others' god or gods. This unique, deified consciousness does not punish or reward anyone. The realization of the personal deified consciousness may set one free from faiths demanding blind following and limiting spiritual choices. Such a spiritual freedom will lead mankind to be one with the physical freedom. A person will no longer feel spiritually alienated from the bazaar economy. That will be a very peaceful co-existence, indeed, between the inner and the outer layers of mankind. It will be good for the economy, too, because spiritually enlightened employees would be more productive when the body, mind and the spirit, all the three, become focused on the basket of goods and services and the meaning of life which is integrated with and, perhaps, which lies beyond the basket of goods and services.

A Historical Perspective

A non religious spiritual quest is not unique to our own times when a need for it is being widely felt. This quest has been going on for as long as mankind has been around. Let's start, then, some five to ten thousand years ago when vedic sages declared thus(Rigved 3:5:5):

कः अद्धावेद कः इह प्रवोचत् देवान् अच्छ पथ्या का समेति
ददृश्रे एषाम् अवमा सदंसि परेषु या गुह्येषु वृतेषु

"Who knows that truth? Who speaks that truth? Who knows and who can declare what pathway leads to the gods? Seen are their lower dwelling places only. What pathway leads to the highest and that which is the most difficult to know?"

This is the way Vedic sages perceived it in their forest ashrams somewhere near the border areas of modern day pre-partition India, Afghanistan and Iran. This is how they thought to summarize the outcome of their spiritual quest while contemplating over their unique and personal pursuit and experience of the cosmic reality and the path or paths leading to that. From a historical perspective, a study of the currently available Sanskrit and Avesthic literature belonging to that period reveals that that was a time of an intense spiritual quest for the people who seem to belong to two groups- Sur (सुर) and Asur (असुर). We do not know with a high degree of certainty whether the Sur people, who were sub-divided into eleven tribes, lived in the eastern geographical areas of Baluchistan and Gandhar, modern day Kandahar, and the Asur people lived in the western part in southern Iran or they lived co-mingled with each other. However, we do know that Indra was the leader of the Sur people and Ahur Mazda (Asur Mahat, in Sanskrit, असुर महत्, meaning the Great Asur) was the leader of the Asur people. The Asur, most likely, were the southern Iranians of the Pars region and, maybe, from areas farther to the south of the Pars region. However, it is also noteworthy that a group of Irani Kurd people speak a language which is called Sorani or Surani, literally meaning, pertaining to Sur.

The spiritual seekers from both groups shared objects of worship like Agni (अग्नि), Varun (वरुण), Mitra (मित्र), Apamnapat(Apam Napat in Avestha), Gandharva(Gandarewa in Avestha), Krishanu(Keresani in Avestha), Vayu, Yama(son of Vivasvant in Veda and the son of Vivahvant in Avestha), Rit (ऋत) and Asha (आशा, Asa in Avestha). Using Agni as a spiritual medium between man and gods, Vedic hotri (होत्रि)

performed Yagya (यज्ञ), while Avesthic Zaotar (होत्रि) performed Yasna, which is the same word as Jasna in modern Farsi. Despite a common spiritual foundation, a study of Avestha and Veda further reveals that, although the Sur and the Asur people were living in a close physical proximity to each other, they were not always on a politically friendly term with each other. There is a strong Vedic-Avesthic literary indication that they were hostile to and afraid of each other. Whereas one group invoked Indra to take care of the 'cow stealing and Yagya-disturbing' Asur, the other group called upon Ahur Mazda, the Great Asur, to protect their home, hearth and cows from the hands of the invading Sur. Despite a common, plural spiritual foundation between the Sur and the Asur people, a socio-political divide seems to have taken place- one around Indra as their leader and the other around Ahur Mazda. In such a socio-economic and political environment, it is, indeed, encouraging to hear vedic sages declare with full humility and openness of mind, "Who knows that truth? Who speaks that truth? Who knows and who can declare what pathway leads to the gods? Seen are their lowest dwelling places only. What pathway leads to the highest and to That which is difficult to know?" कः अद्धावेद कः इह प्रवोचत् देवान् अच्छ पथ्या का समेति ददृश्रे एषाम् अवमा सदंसि परेषु या गुह्येषु व्रतेषु (ऋगवेद,३:५:५)।

It is worthy to note that the socio-economic and political hostility between the Sur and the Asur people does not appear to have resulted in a call for spiritual exclusivity. Rigved speaks highly of Asurs' spiritual powers and so does Avestha speak of Surs' spiritual quest with a reverence. Under the protection of their temporal leaders, Indra and Ahur Mazda, both groups, the Indu people, followers of Indra and later called by Arabs as Hindu ('H' sound seems to have been added to the Arabic alef when written in Arabic), and the Persians, respectively, continued to pray and worship a plurality of spiritual objects like Vayu, Mitra, Agni, Asha and several others. Socio-economic and political aggregation around their respective temporal leaders does not seem to have resulted in a spiritual aggregation around singular gods, one god for each group. That was some time between five thousand and ten thousand years ago.

This plural, spiritual tradition, later on, gave birth to a set of well documented and repeatable processes and techniques of yogic transcendental meditation by which each person can possibly attain spiritual enlightenment in his or her own unique way. It is worth noting that a meditative technique was in fact practised by Buddha, around two thousand and five hundred years ago and, five hundred years after that, by Jesus Christ who practised kabala, which is kaivalya in Sanskrit. The knowledge of kabala meditation was brought to the Arabian peninsula by the three magi from the East. The word magi is same as the word magi in the Pali language and same as the word margi in Sanskrit, meaning a wayfarer, a traveller. The three Indu/Buddhist magi, perhaps, trained Jesus in the practice of kabala which, after his own unique and personal spiritual experience, led him to exclaim, 'The Father and I are One'.

The Spirit of One, thus, was born several thousand years ago and nurtured by different sages and several prominent personalities who sought spiritually unique and personal experiences. These sages and spiritual leaders never told other folks to follow them blindly. They were practitioners of and believers in unique and individual spiritual quest. The Spirit of One' needs to be rekindled again in an age and time when mankind is falling prey to religions which demand blind following with a mob mentality and zealotry.

The Loss Of Spiritual Freedom

Let us fast forward to a time some fifteen hundred to two thousand years ago to a nearby area on the Arabian peninsula. Christianity and Islam, both having their roots in the Abrahamic tradition, appear to be more definite and certain about knowing the truth. Both assert that only their version of the truth and their version of the path, which has been described in and prescribed by their respective holy books, the Bible and the Koran, will lead to the truth. Jesus Christ had to pay for his kabalistically unique experience of spirituality with his own life in the most cruel, inhumane and defenseless way in the prime of his youth. He could not save himself from the blind followers and exclusivist religious zealots around him at that time.

Mohammad, another prophet from the Arabian peninsula, some six hundred years later than Jesus, initially avoided the north-western and western part of the peninsula, for the obvious fear of meeting a potentially devastating hostility, until he gathered enough followers for his exclusivist view of the truth. He looked to the north and to the south for more followers and, as a result, his warriors secured Iraq and Egypt, then, they marched forward farther to the north, to the west and to the east to Iran, Afghanistan, India and to the north to Central Asia. Mohammad and his followers were more successful than Christ's followers, over a comparable period of time, in terms of forcefully winning more converts to their own exclusivist view of the Abrahamic path. This was the birth and the beginning of the first breed of sword-wielding crusaders and jehadis on horsebacks.

For the inheritors of the Sur-Asur tradition of the Vedic-Avesthic view of spirituality which is inclusivist at its core, it may be difficult for many to accept Christianity's and Islam's exclusivist positions. One may wonder what spiritual purpose is served by Biblical commands like, "Thou shalt have none other gods before me. Thou shalt not make thee any graven image or any likeness of any thing that is in heaven above or that is in the earth beneath or that is in the waters beneath the earth: thou shalt not bow down thyself unto them, nor serve them: for I the Lord thy God am a jealous God", (Deuteronomy 5:6-9). How can God be jealous? No one knows. Jealousy is not a godly quality, though.

One may also find it equally hard to explain what spiritual purpose is served by Koranic fatwas like this, "And whoso shall rebel against Allah and his prophet, and shall break His bounds, him shall Allah place in the fire to abide therein for ever; and his shall be a shameful torment (Sura 4:18)" and "The Jews say, 'Ozair is the son of God'; and the Christians say, 'the Messiah is a son of God'. Such the sayings in their mouths! They resemble the sayings of the Infidels of old! Allah do battle with them! How are they misguided (Sura 9:30)". 'Him shall Allah place in the fire to abide therein for ever and his shall be a shameful torment'- how does this go with a merciful Allah?, one could be curious to know about. No one knows. Truth is attribute-less and Allah is neither cruel nor kind, neither good nor bad. That is above all these qualifications.

When one reflects deeply on the Abrahamic construction of a justice dispensing, credit-debit accounting God and Allah, who are somewhere up there, it is hard to avoid thinking that the Christian and Islamist views of God and Allah, respectively, are, fundamentally and, perhaps, irreconcilliably, at philosophical odds with the Vedic-Avesthic construction of pluralistic spiritual paths. This difference in approach should not be viewed in terms of the mystical East versus the un-mystical or less mystical West. It is a basic difference between the inclusivist and pluralist Indo-Persian East, temporally led by Indra and Ahur Mazda, on one side, and the exclusivist and singularist Arabian East, led by Abrahamic ideas. It is the East versus the East because all major spiritual and religious traditions of modern times originate from the East. No other geographical area on the earth, except for the Indo-Persian valleys and plains and the Arabian peninsula, has invented a major and a fundamentally different spiritual or religious path which is currently being practised in large numbers. In a physical environment of shifting sand dunes, it appears that the Abrahamic traditions have sought religious stability by ascribing finality to their revealed words. Theirs' is the way and the only way and those outside of their camps are either heathens or kafers. Jesus and Mohammad may not have intended it that way, though.

On the other hand, in an environment of a relative agrarian stability, the Indo-Persian spiritual traditions under the protection of Indra and Ahur Mazda sought for spiritual dynamism and openness by exhorting their folks to keep seeking and to continue the quest, no matter what god one worships. It was not a blasphemy in the Indo-Persian tradition to worship tens of idols, buts (वृत, भृत), side-by-side in but-khaneh (वृतखाने), in temples.

The point here is not to indulge in a criticism of Abrahamic religions like post-Jesus Christianity and post-Mohammad Islam and their ancient and modern day missionary crusaders and jehadis, respectively. Perhaps, the statements quoted above from the Bible and the Koran were well meaning in the beginning. Alhough they may appear to some to have become far removed from the spiritual experience of their religious leaders. Some people say that all religions are same or similar. This may be the case. However, religion is different from spiritualism. It is important to understand the fundamental difference in the foundational first principles of Indra-Ahuric spiritual traditions and those of Abrahamic religions. Whereas Abraham grandfathered prescriptive, exclusivist and singularist religions, Indra and Ahur Mazda grandfathered subscriptive, inclusivist and pluralist spiritual traditions.

It is very important to understand this difference in order to be able to understand what is happening around us today and, also, to exercise one's freedom of choice to choose a spiritual path without political coersion or monetary inducement. It is important to understand the historicity of the beginning of the loss of the spiritual freedom. It is highly likely that Jesus and Mohammad did have a unique spiritual experience of their own. It is also highly plausible that it may have been a failure of the clergy and mollahs who failed to design or adapt from others a process by which each person could realize one's own transcendent reality, one's own truth in ways which may have helped Jesus and Mohammad in their own spiritual quest. This failure may have led to the birth of blind faiths and blind followers. Certainly, Jesus had experienced his own unique spirituality through kabalistic meditative practices brought and taught to him by the three Indu/Buddhist magi, the wayfarers, who came all the way from India. Such a demonstration of 'The Spirit of One' is the pinnacle of spiritual awakening and experience, which is unique, personal and individualistic. This personal experience may also be the most suited path for the bazaar culture of modern times.

The Freedom Of Spiritual Choice

As we begin the journey in the twenty first century, each of us is confronting a situation which calls for making a choice. And the choice to be made is between Abrahamic prescriptive, exclusive and singularist religions and the Indra-Ahuric subscriptive, inclusive and pluralist spiritual traditions of the Indus and the pre-Islamic Persians on the other. Regardless of the choice made or not made, every man's and every woman's mind must remain scientifically and spiritually open, inquisitive and curious. Each person must seek tirelessly. All closed-ended answers to the ancient, spiritual quest of mankind must be opened, re-opened, questioned and questioned again. In this age and time, a religion claiming to know and claiming to be in the exclusive possession of the ultimate truth must be doubted and, perhaps, strongly suspected. Proponents of and adherents to such exclusivist religious clubs must be inquisitively questioned on the validity of their claims.

The issue of having the sole ownership of the 'Truth' is not an issue of a blind faith as some purvey it to be and, thus, try to keep it outside the realm of inquisitive questioning and an intelligent debate. On the other hand, it is an issue of paramount importance to mankind, not only from a spiritual diversity point of view but also from a true freedom of choice point of view. Being simplistically seductive and, therefore, within the intellectual reach of millions of people, closed-ended answers to the spiritual quest of mankind limit the freedom of choice. They limit the growth of spiritual democracy and they, unintentionally, perhaps, attempt to destroy spiritual diversity which every human being is entitled to. 'The Spirit of One' is a birth right for all of mankind. To oppose, through dialogue, debate and discourse, prescriptive, exclusivist, singularist, closed-ended, 'my god is the only god' and 'my path is the only path' kind of religious zealotry must become a duty of each man and each woman. Everyone, following one's own path, has the inner seed of seeking and finding one's own spiritual end, one's own god. That god, which one will, thus, find, does not necessarily have to be a likeness of others' gods.

Therefore, in a spiritual context, construction and communication of statements like, 'if you are not with us, you are against us', 'if you are not a Christian, you will go to hell unless saved by Christ's caring couriers' and 'if you do not follow Pagambar's preachings you are condemned to a perpetual perdition' could be assumed to have been crafted in a mind which is spiritually unenlightened, dishonest, disinclined and, perhaps, intolerant and belligerent. Some may brand such a viewpoint in a modern-day context as an act of spiritually debilitating devilry. It is an act against 'The Spirit of One'; it is an act against the freedom of spiritual choice. Such a threatening point of view is against the spiritual plurality sought and promoted by ancient Indus, the Persians, the Greeks and the Egyptians. Moreover, such views militate against the very foundation of those nations which have organized themselves around the concepts of freedom, democracy and the bazaar economy where individual uniqueness and achievement are worshipped and celebrated.

Whereas Greece, Egypt and Persia fell, long time ago, to the swords of religious zealots, India is the only surviving nation, today, whose soul, though sufficiently shaken and, perhaps, militantly aroused by a persistent Abrahamic assault, even in our own times, is still rooted in the plural Vedic-Avesthic spiritual traditions. India's plural soul must be nourished, preserved, protected and defended by all who believe in unique spiritual realization for each person on the planet against the militating or proselytising Abrahamic singularist jehadis and missionaries. The defense of the plural derives its sustaining strength from the fundamental principle of spiritual diversity. And, to maintain this diversity, let not the Indian Lakshmi go the way of the Persian Asa; let not the Indian Saraswati go the way of the Greek Athena- right into oblivion. Let's have a jasna around Agni for the Plural; let everyone bring their own gods, their own buts and their own idols for the jasna; let everyone celebrate the spiritual diversity of mankind in all its radiant and transcendent glory.

Towards The Spirit Of One

The concept of plural spirituality leads one to the question: how many gods are there, anyway? Another question can be asked: how many gods can possibly be out there in this world and in the worlds beyond? How many gods should there be? An answer, which appears simplistic in its formulation but bears a more complex and sophisticated spiritual import, could, theoretically, be given as such: there are, potentially, as many gods existent, at a point in time, as there are human beings on this earth and beyond. Another question could be asked: what about other life forms, like animals and plants? A possible response to this question could be: Why not? So, how many gods are there or could be there? One response could be: There were billions of gods before and there are billions of gods now and there will be billions of gods tomorrow. Interestingly, a similar question was posed, in Brihad-Aranyak Upanishad, by Shakalya to Yagyavalkya, "How many gods are there, Yagyavalkya?" This question had evoked a conceptually similar response: 'there are three hundred and three gods and three thousand and three…….. , then, there are three gods,……… then, there is one and half……., then, there is one', proclaimed rishi Yagyavalkya. 'And, that One is You', adds The Spirit of One. Such a response gives rise to a practical problem: how does one manage such an apparently chaotic and possibly bewildering spiritual diversity, where everyone is a seeker and everyone could possibly find one's own god? One possible answer could be: there is no need to manage a person's spiritual quest, which is inherently limitless and, perhaps, un-ending; there is no need to organize spirituality into religio-political groupings with administrators, bureaucrats and missionaries. The 'Spirit of One' is what needs to be practised. What is needed is a series of steps and a repeatable, spiritual process so that each one of us can experience the spiritual awakening, the way Indu sages did; the way Buddha did; the way Jesus did.

In this regard, Persians, perhaps, have a clever resolution when they use the word khoda for God and khodi for self. One might wonder why a spiritual quest cannot result in having one khoda for each khodi or, perhaps, several khodas for each khodi? In author's view, there is no theoretical limit on the number of khodas and if each khodi discovers a khoda for itself, no laws of physics will be broken. Therefore, let's keep seeking that which is the inner core of each man and each woman.

As the vedic rishi wondered loud, "Whence did these various created beings appear, who created them or who did not create them- all this is known to only That. Or, maybe, even That does not know (सः अंग वेद यदि वा न वेद)". No one can be sure, beyond doubt, whether there is a God or not or whether there is an Allah or not. No one can, similarly, be sure about one's assertion that the authorship of this universe rests with God or Allah. No one can say without raising suspicion that if you do not follow my God you will not be 'saved' and you will go to hell. And, with that sense of uncertainty and skepticism, then, each of us is an inquisitive non-believer or a kafer.

However, we know, for sure, that each person has five sense organs- eyes, ears, nose, tongue and skin- through which a person collects information about form, sound, smell, taste and touch, respectively, from the external world. We also know that each of us has a mouth, two hands, two feet and two excretory organs(one of which doubles as a procreative organ) through which important and critical bodily functions are performed. We also know that there is something called mind, which is itself an aggregate of several things including brain, which supervises/controls the functioning of these organs. We also know that there is a discriminative aspect of human thinking called intellect and there is, then, a stage in thinking which is commonly called the wisdom. That which is beyond

A Spiritual Model
Figure 1.0

wisdom and that which is the object of spiritual seeking is what is variously called the atman, the roh, the self, the spirit, i.e., the inner core of a man and a woman. This has been shown in Figure 1.0.

That inner core must be sought and realized through knowledge by each person individually as the Vedic rishis did and as Jesus did when he declared, "The Father and I are One". The process of seeking and realizing that inner core, that atman, that roh, that khodi and that personal god is too important a process to be left at the mercy of a blind faith or at the mercy of someone else's revealed words. 'The Spirit of One' is a vision for the scientific and rationalist context in which repeatability of a process is very important. A repeatability of a process also lends scalability and, thus, does not get constrained by the availability of pagambars, prophets, padres, pastors and priests. God is in all of us and each of us has a piece of Allah. Each man and each woman has to come to this realization through intelligent searching within. Therefore, to be called a heathen, a pagan, a non-believer or a kafer should not be paid attention to.

Let everyone be a seeker. Let every home become a temple; let every heart become a temple; let every home harbour its own god; let every heart harbour its own god; let everyone be spiritually free; let everyone have limitless spiritual choices; let everyone follow their own spiritual quest without interference of any kind from religio-political groupings. Let every man and woman, at the end of one's own unique and un-replicable spiritual journey, proclaim, "I am That, अहम् ब्रह्मास्मि, I am God, The Father and I are One, I am Allah and man khoda hastam. Let each khodi realize, in its own unique way, a transcension beyond its temporal cage and become one with the time-transcendent khoda. There are no non-believers. There are no kafers. All are believers. All will believe in their own miraculous powers after they realize their god within.

Uniqueness is individual; uniqueness is freedom; uniqueness is beautiful; uniqueness is godly; uniqueness is sacred and pure. Spiritual uniqueness of a man and a woman is a precondition for individual uniqueness. All who rob an individual of one's spiritual uniqueness are acting against individuality; they are acting against freedom; they are acting against beauty; they are acting against godliness and they are acting against purity. They cannot, imaginably, be working as God's agents. Such people and such institutions must be peacefully confronted and debated with. Prevention of the spiritual destruction of the diseased and the destitute must be the foundation for a true freedom of seeking, for a true freedom of spirituality. The world must move away from enacting laws for 'Freedom of Religion' and evolve to legislating laws for 'Freedom of Spirituality'.

The Agenda: Preservation Of The Plural

'The Spirit of One' has been written with the spiritual agenda of promoting and preserving spiritual uniqueness of each person in the world through selected spiritual dialogues from India. The seeds of these dialogues, largely, originated, as has been noted before, from around the geographical areas of pre-partition India, modern day Afghanistan and Iran, some time between five and ten thousand years ago. Although, people from modern day Iran, Afghanistan and the north-western part of pre-partition India have become the followers of Islam, a persistent stirring, emanating from the souls of these people, who were converted to Islam during the last fourteen hundred years, can be discerned even today. When one muses over the poems of Jallalludin Rumi who was an Afghani; when one listens to sufi songs, ghazals and qawwalis from these lands, painfully capturing, through their plaintive strain, khodi's yearning to seek and unite with its khoda, one cannot avoid feeling that the core of the Irani, Afghani and pre-partition north-western Indian people is still Vedic-Avesthic at heart despite their Islamization over the centuries. The search for plurality and the quest for spiritual diversity is being manifested in the form of political struggles in these countries even in our own times. It appears that the ancient, Vedic-Avesthic, spiritual diversity of these lands is in a state of perseverent confrontation with the singular and rigorous requirements of Islamic theology. In all these nations, the Abrahamic singularist viewpoint, from the East, is in a philosophical struggle with the Vedic-Avesthic, Indo-Persian pluralistic approach, which is also from the East. No wonder, then, that the maximum number of variations of Islam, including Shia, Sufi, Ahmadia, Ismaili and Bahai, to name a few, have originated from these lands and not from the Arabian peninsula.

It is the author's hope, then, that the spiritual dialogues, which have been culled from the vedic tradition and presented and commented upon in this book, will help preserve and promote the Indu spiritual diversity and plurality. It is hoped that the spiritual quest of a man or a woman will result in finding one's own god. And if, by chance or through a persevering effort, a man or a woman reaches at the same spiritual end as others before, that, too, is as great and as beautiful.

Let the dialogues begin, then.

The Ten Spirits of One

Although there are literally thousands of spiritual dialogues recorded and available, even today, in Sanskrit texts, only ten of them have been selected for discussion in this book. It was indeed a difficult task to cull these ten dialogues out of so many, however, an effort was made to cover a wide spectrum of spiritual guidance available through a select few, which illustrate the principle behind and the process of 'The Spirit of One' more clearly.

The first dialogue, between Arjun and Krishna, has been taken from the Bhagavad Gita and is rooted in the upanishadic tradition, which evolved from the vedic spirituality. Arjun and Krishna were generational peers, therefore, this is a spiritual journey of a man led by his peer and a friend. Arjun is beset with a critical decision- whether to fight in a war or not. He, along with his brothers and allies, is facing his own cousins, teachers, grand uncles, grand parents and their allies, on the other side, in the battlefield. Arjun's expressed reluctance to fight in the war leads Krishna to take Arjun on a spiritual journey of self-discovery and that, too, in a real-life and real-time battlefield. The spiritual journey starts with an understanding of the temporal nature of man and ends with a realization of the time transcendent core of the man. Arjun realizes that the time transcendent core of his own existence is an emanation of the time transcendent cosmic reality. This is the longest dialogue in the book and has been structured around sixteen questions Arjun has asked Krishna in the battlefield of Kurukshetra.

The second dialogue takes place between a husband, Yagyavalkya, and his wife, Maitreyi, in Brihad-Aranyak Upanishad. It happens that Yagyavalkya was also a great spiritual teacher of his times. The context is like this: Yagyavalkya is ready to leave his duties as a householder and is ready to retire to the forest for the third stage in life, vanaprastha (वानप्रस्थ). Before he sets forth on his journey to the forests, he calls Maitreyi and tells her about his desire to renounce worldly attachments and about his plan to go to the forest. Before he does that, he wants to divide his worldly possessions between his two wives, Maitreyi and Katyayani. Upon hearing her husband's plans, Maitreyi askes him a question, "What should I do with that wealth by which I will not become immortal?" Yagyavalkya, then, takes his wife, Maitreyi, on her own unique spiritual journey.

The dialogue between Yama and Nachiketa, which is the third one in this book, has been taken from Kath Upanishad, which belongs to the taitariya school of Yajurved. The story of Yama and Nachiketa has been, for the first time, mentioned in the Rigved (10:135). Nachiketa, along with two other questions, asks Yama, "Tell me the way to conquer punah-mrityu, re-death. This question is conceptually similar to the one posed by Maitreyi. Nachiketa and Maitreyi, both, want to discover whether there is something which is time transcendent and, therefore, which outlives the temporal manifestation in this world or not. Yama leads Nachiketa to his own unique spiritual discovery.

The fourth dialogue in this book is between Narad (नारद) and Sanatkumar (सनत्कुमार) and has been selected from Chhandogya Upanishad, which belongs to the Samved. Narad, a great rishi of all times, goes to Sanatkumar, who was born of Dharma (धर्म) and Ahimsa (अहिंसा) as his father and mother, respectively. Sanatkumar has been depicted as an eternal, five year old child in Indian spiritual books symbolizing eternal inquisitiveness. Narad asks a question, "Venerable Sir, is there anything beyond a name? Tell that to me." This is a loaded, yet a simple, question. What Narad wants to know is whether there is a Roh, an Atman, or not. Sanatkumar shares his spiritual discovery with Narad and takes him, layer-by-layer and step-by-step, to the core of the man.

The dialogue between Balaki and Ajatshatru has been taken from Brihad-Aranyak Upanishad. Balaki, of the Gargya genealogy, was a boastful Brahmin preacher. Although he spent most of his time worshipping the sun and the moon and other natural objects, he boasted of having a very good knowledge of the Brahman (बृह्मन्). He offers to share his spiritual knowledge with Ajatshatru who was the king of Kashi, the modern day Varanasi in India. This dialogue presents a progressive definition of Brahman.

This dialogue, between Valikhilyas and Prajapati, was narrated by rishi Shakayanya (शाकायन्य) to king Brihadrath (बृहदरथ), who was a descendent of the king Ikshvaku (ईक्ष्वाकु). This has been taken from Maitri Upanishad, which belongs to the maitrayaniya branch of the Krishna Yajur Ved. Rishi Maitri was the founder of this branch of rishis which Shakayanya belonged to. The dialogue captures the spiritual quest of a king as Shakayanya tells Brihadrath, "Now, indeed, O King, this is the knowledge about Brahman.......as declared to us by revered Maitri......I will narrate it to you". Shakayanya, then, goes on narrating the dialogue between Valikhilyas and Prajapati.

This next dialogue takes place at a meeting of several rishis where Yagyavalkya is the chief guest. The meeting place is an ashram somewhere in the Brihad Aranya, literally, the great forest and, thus, this dialogue has been taken from the Brihad-Aranyak Upanishad. Several rishis have already asked their questions and now it is the turn of Vachaknavi Gargi, who gets up and addresses her peers, "Venerable Brahmins, I will ask him two questions. If he answers them both, then, none of you will succeed in defeating him in the debate about Brahman". Gargi's peers, in unison, said, "Ask them, Gargi". Gargi turned to Yagyavalkya and said, "Yagyavalkya, that which is in the sky, that which is on the earth, that which is in between the earth and the sky and that which the people call the past, the present and the future, the Time, what is the underlying unity behind all these?"

The background for the eighth dialogue is exactly the same as the one between Gargi and Yagyavalkya, same ashram in the same great forest and the same rishis gathered together to listen to and ask questions to Yagyavalkya. It is the turn of a rishi called Shakalya (शकल्य), who asked, "How many gods are there, Yagyavalkya?"

Yagyavalkya responds, "As many as are mentioned in the invocation of the gods, namely, three hundred and three, and three thousand and three". Yagyavalkya, ultimately and progressively, takes Shakalya to the realization of the spiritual core of this universe.

The ninth dialogue has been taken from the Chhandogya Upanishad and captures the spiritual quest of Satyakam (सत्यकाम), a man of a very humble beginning and upbringing, with the help from Gautam (गौतम), a rishi and the son of Haridrumat(this Gautam is not the same Gautam, the Buddha). Actually, a large part of the dialogue takes place between Satyakam and several animals, fire and a cow-bull, named Rishabh. Satyakam, filled with a strong desire for understanding the nature of the ultimate reality, went to his mother, Jabala (जवाला) and asked her, "Mother, I want to live a life of a Brahmachari, a student seeking spiritual knowledge. Of what family tree, of what gotra, am I from?" Thus begins Satyakam's unique and fascinating spiritual journey.

The last dialogue takes place between a father, Varun (वरुण), and his son, Bhrigu (भृगु). It has been taken from Taitariya Upanishad, which belongs to the taitariya school of Yajur Ved. The dialogue starts with a simple, candid and blunt question from the son to his father, "Sir, teach me about Brahman (अधीहि भगवो ब्रह्मा इति)". Varun tells his son, 'matter, life, sight, hearing, mind and speech (अन्नम् प्राणम् चक्षुश श्रोत्रम् मनः वाचम् इति)' and lets Bhrigu self-discover by repeatedly saying to him, 'contemplate' in response to questions from him.

A Mini Epilogue: The Vision

As one goes through each dialogue, one is bound to come to a conclusion that nothing has been revealed by anyone to anyone, whether it is Krishna or Yagyavalkya or Yama or Varun or someone else. A strong message, which is repeatedly received from these dialogues, is that each man and each woman has to seek their own reality in their own unique way. Whether that reality is god or khoda or khodi or roh or atman or brahman or self or nothing, it is upto the individual seeker to seek it out. Once that seeking is done, then, the seeker becomes one with that which was being sought- khodi becomes khoda, atman becomes brahman, the biblical Father and the Son become one, man becomes god and woman becomes goddess. At that point, when This and That dissolve into one, the sufi stops singing; the kaivalya seeker stops seeking and the qawwali singer stops rendering qawwalis. The knower and the knowledge, the seeker and the sought, the singer and the song, the subject and the object and the lover and the beloved- each one of a pair becomes one and indistinguishable from the other in each pair. Each can rightfully proclaim, with a great degree of spiritual satisfaction, 'man khoda hastam, I am God, I am Allah, अहम् ब्रह्मास्मि.

This vision of 'The Spirit of One' has no non-believers. There are no pagans. There are no heathens. There are no kafers. All will go to heaven, that is, if there is a heaven. Certainly, no one will go to hell, that is, if there is one. 'The Spirit of One' does not need anyone to save anyone. No one who cannot save one's own self maybe qualified to save anyone else's, anyway. Each one of us is our own saviour. That's the Indra-Ahuric wisdom of the Plural. 'The Spirit of One' has the potential and the promise of closing the chasm between a person's physical world and the spiritual world. 'The Spirit of One' offers the possibility of removing the spiritual anomie from the bazaar economy. Along with one's own unique basket of one's own unique goods and services in the bazaar, let everyone bring one's own idols. Let everyone bring one's own buts. Let everyone bring one's own gods.

When the goods and the gods are all unique, the world will be at peace. A mob goes to war, not an individual.

Let the spiritual safar, the journey, begin.

Kamalesh Dwivedi
Eden Prairie, MN, USA
Year-2003